KEEP MOVING FORWARD

My Marathon Des Sables Journey

Duncan Nealon

CONTENTS

To my wife, Lucy; without whom none of this would have been possible. To my children, Millie and Ted; without whom this would have been pointless. To my mum who means more to me than she'll ever know. And to my dad, Brian Patrick Joseph; it would all be so much more fun if you were here to enjoy it too. I love you all dearly.

Dream on
Dream on
Dream on
Dream until your dreams come true...

Steven Tyler

CHAPTER 1

Silence; punctuated by my footsteps and the rhythm of my steady breathing. It's just turned 1am. I've been on my feet for over 16 hours and I'm struggling. Technically speaking, I hit 'the wall' a few hours ago and have been running on empty since. I feel hollow inside, like my soul is being both emptied, and bared for the world to see. My feet are causing me serious issues. I can tell that I have blisters on both heels, and each time I put my left foot down in a certain position, it feels like I am standing on a drawing pin. I enter the checkpoint, keen to maintain sight of the competitors who have entered just ahead of me. Knowing they are there offers some comfort amidst the darkness.

I sit on the rug in one of the medical tents and start pulling at my gaiter to free up my shoe laces. I'm not thinking straight and can't seem to undo the laces. One of the Doc Trotter team comes over to me and asks me what the problem is. I explain, in a combination of broken French and English that I need to strap my feet. I ask them if they can help, but they politely tell me this isn't allowed and that I must do it myself. I try to light-heartedly plead with them, but they remain firm. I begin to tape my feet, but I can't manoeuvre my legs into the right position to do it properly and make a bit of a hash of it. The Doctor watches on impassively. Just as I finish putting my shoes back on, I realise that I have put them on ahead of my gaiters, meaning I must take them off and start over. 'For fuck's sake,' I chuckle to myself; at least I'm still laughing... Eventually I am ready, with my makeshift taping, and my trainers and gaiters in place. But at this exact moment I suddenly begin shaking violently. 'What the hell's the matter with me?' I think. Then my teeth start to chatter to an almost comedic extent. I hear the Doctor say something about 'hypothermia' and say she is going to get someone. I don't want this. I don't want her to get anyone. Someone else may say something I don't want to hear. Something like 'you must wait here until you warm up.' So I grab my down jacket from my bag, a small bag of M&Ms and Haribo that I had made up back in the UK, and do my best to get out of the checkpoint as quickly as I can, whilst the Doctor is searching for someone to come and look at me.

I know what the problem is, and it's not serious. I just sat down stationary for too long and have got a bit cold which, combined with very low blood sugar wasn't a particularly clever idea. I have 10km to go. By my calculations this will take me approximately two hours. The idea of taking two hours to complete 10km both amuses and infuriates me. I put my head down and settle back into my slow but determined rhythm. My fellow competitors I hoped to stay attached to are long gone when I exit the check point, and I find myself in no-mans-land. I can see no-one ahead of me, with no-one yet coming up behind. It is pitch black other than the bobbing of my head-torch. Above me is the most incredible starscape. I stare upwards as I move, mesmerised by the view. The sky is so clear in the desert, and the view is unlike anything I have ever seen before. Yet not looking where I am going causes me to kick a large rock with my toe. With blisters under my toenails, this is far from ideal, and I remind myself that at this stage, this isn't a sight-seeing expedition, and I need to focus on getting the job done.

It is eerily quiet. I've long since packed away my headphones. With precious little vision in the dark, I feel the need to maximise my other senses. Yet in the middle of the Sahara Desert there is very little wildlife, and as such barely any sound. My soundtrack is the rhythmic noise of my feet hitting the ground. In the soft sand however, my feet are making very little noise; or maybe I am just too tired to hear it. Either way, I am moving in an almost trance like state with little visual or audio backdrop. This is playing with my head; it's almost like I am on a silent treadmill in a dark room. Am I actually getting anywhere?

An hour and a half later and I catch a glimpse of the finish line; marked by the usual inflatable gantry, with floodlights all around. I weigh up how far away it appears to sit. Not that far, I reckon. Maybe I will get there in less than half an hour? But the desert plays with your mind. It always makes things appear closer than they actually are. There's no point debating it though. I redouble my efforts and try to break into a jog. It lasts approximately 20 seconds before fatigue forces me back into my march. Gradually, I get closer to the lights of the finish. I feel I am probably one mile away. Just one mile. That is the same as my house to the edge of the village we live just outside. I run that as a warm up. Surely I can run it in? I try again to run, but once more I am forced to settle back into a march. Then, all of a sudden, I hear chatter behind me. I look back and see between six and ten head-torches. Shit! There's a group approaching me, and from the sounds of things, they're going to overtake me. My position within the pack isn't that important to me in itself, but I'm buggered if I'm going to be pipped at the finish by a load of people who have been using me as a homing beacon. I know that at home my wife will be tracking me online, and quite possibly watching the live webcam to see me finish. I am filled with a foolish sense of macho pride. I don't want her to see me overtaken at the end of this monumental struggle. So I force myself into a run. And all of a sudden, it turns out I can run; I am running quite quickly in fact! I look at my Strava app on my phone (my watch has long since gone flat) and I am running at 8 minute mile pace. Not exactly record breaking, but the quickest I have travelled all week. Yet each step is a struggle and my body is imploring me to revert to a walk. I won't allow it though; terrified that the voices I can hear behind will catch me. They don't however, and in fact, I am building quite a gap between me and them. All of a sudden, I notice that not only have I left that group behind, but I have also overtaken another group of three, moving approximately thirty metres to my left, that I had thus far not noticed. A few minutes later and I am running into the funnel, and across the line.

A warm smile greets me from the official manning the line. 'Well done!' she shouts in her French accent. (She can see I am British from my race number). I muster up the energy to fake high-spirits and enthusiasm. 'Merci beaucoup! Comment allez-vous?!' I chirp back. Then I remember the webcam. I walk back in front of it, blow my cheeks out and mouth 'that was tough.' Then I wonder what the hell I am playing at and self-consciously walk through to the water station. I am not emotional, as I thought I would be. Nor am I triumphant. I am just calm and accepting.

I have just completed the challenge that has been causing me anxiety and stress for the last two years. I have just succeeded at the task that has indirectly caused me to be short with my wife for no reason; to be impatient with my kids unfairly; to lose concentration in work meetings at the drop of the hat; and to spend hour after hour pounding the pavements and hammering the treadmill. I have just completed the 52 miles that makes up the long stage of the Marathon Des Sables.

CHAPTER 2

vividly remember the first time I heard of the Marathon Des Sables. It was autumn 1998 and I was living in Sheffield as a student. I was twenty years old and had been a reasonable schoolboy athlete. Not exactly sensational, but competitive and worth my place on the team. I was reading Athletics Weekly and there was a short article on the event. It was described almost as a novelty event at that stage, however the article contained one key descriptor – 'the toughest footrace on earth.' That line alone alighted something in me that meant I knew – and I do mean, *knew*, that one day, I would take on the challenge. If someone was going to describe an event as the toughest footrace on earth, that was asking a question of me that I knew I had to find the answer to. I turned to the person I was with, flicking ash from my cigarette into an empty beer can, and said

'I'm going to run this one day.' They didn't even bother to feign interest, and I continued leafing through the magazine. I can't remember when the MDS next entered my consciousness, but it was some considerable time later. What was clear though, looking back, was that at that precise moment, a tiny fire was lit in the back of my head that would eventually come to grow to a point where I could no longer ignore it.

The label 'Toughest Footrace on Earth' was quite probably accurate when the Discovery Channel first offered it to the Marathon Des Sables, however it is clear that over the years, this title has become a little hyperbolic. Many other races such as the Barkley Marathons, the Jungle Ultra, the Yukon and Comrades, could very justifiably claim to be 'tougher' than the MDS. Yet the MDS remains the Grand-daddy of Ultras. The best-known multi-stage ultra, and the one best serving as a common currency amongst runners. At trail races, you will often here people muttering 'he's done the MDS you know' in hushed tones, whilst nodding towards a now God-like figure in the distance.

The history of the MDS is inspiring in itself. The race was the brainchild of French concert promoter Patrick Bauer who, in 1984 made a lone voyage through the Sahara. He did so on foot, and on his own, covering 350 km (214 miles) in 12 days. Two years later in 1986 the first Marathon des Sables was run. Twenty-three runners participated in the first race and by 2009 over 1,000 runners participated in the event. An MDS finishers medal remains the property of a very exclusive club. To put it into perspective, in 2015, Runners World estimated that 18,000 people had completed it. In 2017, 40,382 people completed the London Marathon. So over double the number of MDS finishers *ever*, completed the London Marathon in one year. And the London isn't even the biggest marathon in the world; in 2017 over 50,000 people completed the New York Marathon. Yes, the MDS is very niche, and very special.

A self-supported race, where you must carry everything you need for the week, the Marathon Des Sables is a multi-stage ultra-marathon. Competitors carry literally everything they require for the week on their back. The only exceptions being the tents to sleep in, and water which is given at regular intervals – even then, however, you carry water with you on the course. The course varies each year, however the distances travelled are typically consistent year on year. The 2018 course was to look like this:

Day 1	30.3KM
Day 2	39.0KM
Day 3	31.6KM
Day 4	86.2KM
Day 5	Rest day (or complete Day4)
Day 6	42.4KM
Day 7	7.7KM

The temperature in the desert regularly exceeds 50°C, and there are sandstorms galore. If you Google "Marathon Des Sables" one of the first suggestions Google will offer you is "Marathon Des Sables Deaths," which says it all really. The MDS isn't for the faint of heart, nor mind. And that is the whole point.

Close to two decades would pass between me first reading of the MDS and lining up on the start line. Those decades were full of what was fairly normal, if fairly outlandish behaviour. I partied my way through my student years before graduating and embarking on 'adult life' with a tongue very firmly in my cheek. I teamed back up with my local rugby club, Claverdon RFC. We played at a pretty low level, and I was one of the weaker players, but the fun was good, the beer was plentiful, and the laughs were loud. I actually attempted the London marathon in 2003. I barely trained however, and endured a very painful 'race' before staggering over the line in around 4h45m.

Lucy and I got married in 2007 and we enjoyed our early years of newly married freedom; working hard; playing harder and generally having a ball. In 2010 I was over the moon when Lucy ran downstairs waving a positive pregnancy test at me. It was, as any parent knows, the most incredible news. We couldn't wait to tell our respective parents who were just as delighted as we were. Lucy's parents were already grandparents however mine weren't. My dad seemed particularly excited at the prospect of his ensuing grand-fatherhood.

Very sadly, however, only a few months later, our family was rocked by the death of my dad. It was entirely unexpected. He had a heart attack whilst leaving their home for work when he was aged only 66. Part of what was so shocking was that he was in great physical condition (or so we thought). He still ran and swam regularly, and wasn't carrying any excess weight. His untimely death seemed so unbelievably unfair to me. Having left school at 14, he had been working hard his whole life to provide well for his family. He'd been so excited and proud of the thought of a grandchild to love and watch grow. I remember walking down the aisle in the church at his funeral, looking at Lucy who was heavily pregnant, thinking 'how can this be right? How is this fair?' There's no such thing as 'fair' in life though, so I tried to console myself with the fact that at least he had known about the grandchild on the way. That was something, at least.

My dad was a huge fan of running and athletics in general, and a massive influence on my life. He passed his love of athletics onto me. I remember him pacing out in the garden, the exact distance that Bob Beamon had jumped in 1968, and my disbelief when I saw the superhuman distance involved. He brought me up on tales of Vladimir Kuts, Emil Zátopek, Seb Coe, Daley Thompson & Dave Moorcroft. He loved it, and I took his passion for the sport to an even higher level. I could, and still can, name the evolution of most athletics' world records. My friends often mock my 'statto' knowledge of all things athletics. Simply put though, I love it. The simplicity of testing how fast, far and high the human body can move fascinates me to the extreme.

Sadly, when my dad died all thoughts of sport had to be put on hold however, as circumstance insisted I take responsibility for the family forklift truck business alongside my own separate marketing insight business. This was a very tough decision as the pressure of running the two businesses was obviously going to be significant. As it was, we had many people working for the business who had worked for our family for 30 or so years, so I felt we owed it to them to maintain as much consistency as possible. We could have sold the business straightaway (someone even put an offer on the business in a condolence card to my mother 2 days after my dad's death!) but I felt to do so would be to sell my dad short. I had always had the utmost admiration for what my dad had built up from scratch and I wasn't about to let some vultures opportunistically take advantage of circumstance. So we pushed ahead.

I would work 15 hour days routinely, week in, week out. I would work the forklift business during the day, and arrive home, fire up my laptop and start on the marketing side of things. Ultimately, the pressure and associated lack of time saw me put on quite a bit of weight. People have different ways of dealing with grief. I think I ate my way through mine and put on probably 2 ½ stone more than I needed.

In the middle of this darkest of times however, our daughter, Millie May was born. Millie's arrival was quite genuinely, the most incredible event of my life. All parents feel like this, I realise, however Millie arrived into the middle of an extremely dark period (it's only now, with a few years perspective on it that I realise just *how* dark) and served as a light of hope. She was incredible. I had never seen something so perfect in my life. And she hit the ground running in terms of endearing herself to her parents. She slept through, from 7pm until 8am literally every single day from 6 weeks old until she was about 18 months. I remember once saying to a babysitter, 'if she wakes up, we've no idea what you should do, because she's never woken up before!' She very quickly developed a filthy laugh, and clearly had a great sense of fun. I was totally smitten, and it was largely because of her that, in 2013, I joined a gym, and got myself both trim, and fit. I lost the weight I'd put on, toned up, and thought I'd get my running shoes back out.

I just started with the cliched 'running around the block' but soon ventured a bit further. It felt so good to be running again! As over-dramatic as it sounds, it was like I had rediscovered a part of myself I had long forgotten. One day, I saw an advert for the Kenilworth Half Marathon so thought I would enter. Lucy asked me beforehand what I was hoping for and I coyly confessed that I was hoping for a sub 90min half. It's a reasonably hilly course, but I managed to get round in 1h28m which pleased me no end.

The process of losing weight and getting fit was an interesting one. I'd always, naïvely, and rather arrogantly, thought that gym work didn't really have much impact on me. I'd also assumed that I could eat, pretty much, what I wanted. What I learned pretty fast was that the quickest way to sort your physical shape out, was to reduce and improve your food intake. There was a sign in the gym that said 'abs are made in the kitchen, not the gym.' I'm sure this sign must exist in gyms across the land, yet I was amazed that it had taken me to the age of 36 to work it out! How ridiculous. But once I'd worked it out, I lost 2 ½ stone in 12 weeks, and feeling in better shape became addictive. I then learned two further things; firstly, that it is far easier to stay in shape than it is to *get in* shape. If you're in shape, and have a bit of a blow out weekend, you can redress the balance pretty quickly, provided you've got a handle on what's going on. The second, and this has become one of the most valuable things I've learned about myself, is that my will power finds it easier to make myself do things I don't want to do, than stop myself from doing things I *do* want to do.

I'd battled with this dilemma without properly understanding it for years. As a student, I didn't mind pulling all-nighters in order to get my assignments done if the timings necessitated it. Equally however, I'd struggle to say 'no' to something that sounded fun even if my schedule didn't really allow it. The fact that the latter behaviour typically forced the former is not lost on me! The behaviour continued into adulthood. As a young professional I wasn't earning very much money yet lived like I was. My spending stayed the same and through hard work and the odd bit of luck, my earning eventually caught up. Simply put, unbeknown to me, I'd developed a life technique of managing one excess with another. Spend too much? Earn more. Eat too much? Run more. It's quite probably not the best life tactic, but once I'd actually noticed it as a behavioural trait, it became a useful technique for managing my life.

A year or so after getting myself in better shape, our daughter was joined by a son. Ted was a bundle of trouble and hi-jinx from the start. He was just as perfect as his sister, but in a very different way. Weighing in at 9lbs10oz, he was a right chunk and I was over the moon to have a son to play with. As we adjusted to life as a family of four, I put fitness on the back burner for a little while, before dialling up the heat a touch, in search of a sub 3 hour marathon.

A sub-3 marathon was achieved following some intensive and dedicated training, wrapped up in a 16 week plan that I designed myself. (16 weeks was probably a little too long, truth be known.) A sub-3 hour marathon had become a goal after hearing Steve Cram commentate on a London Marathon, and proclaiming *'if these runners coming up The Mall now put some effort in, they may sneak under the 3 hour mark. Sub 3 hours; that's when you start getting respect in the marathon world.'*

I managed to clock a 2hr58m marathon time and a year or so later sped up a bit in my quest for a quick London Marathon. I ran a 1h19m half-marathon but then pretty much instantly injured myself and had to pull out of London.

As I convalesced, and seeing myself now as a reasonable fun-runner, able to be a bit of a pain in the arse to the more serious club runners around me, my thoughts returned to the MDS. To be honest, they had never really left it. It was just now I started to feel like I had a chance of pursuing the dream. Or at the very least, I felt that I had earned the chance to at least consider the possibility of attempting it. The truth is, I still felt it was at the absolute extremities of my dreams.

My aspirations hit a bit of a bump in the road, when we went on holiday to Cyprus. I went out for a run during the heat of the day and my thermostat blew. I just couldn't handle the oppressive heat. Upon returning to our villa I dived straight into our pool, fully clothed before getting out, sitting down and feeling very despondent. There was just no way I could cope with the heat. It was a very sobering, devastating moment. I'd harboured dreams of conquering the desert for nearly 20 years, but the harsh reality of the Cyprus heat had showed me that I just wasn't up to dealing with the conditions. I sat quietly by the poolside for a few minutes, trying to process things. Simply put, there was no way that I could deal with this level of heat whilst running long distances. The temperature in Cyprus was around 36c, whilst there were reports of the temperatures in the desert hitting 50c. The basic maths didn't make for pleasant reading.

When I returned from holiday, I gave the matter some more thought, again trying to process the situation. One thought kept returning to my head... If other people can do it, why can't I? After months of deliberation and consideration, I realised a subtle yet crucial thing; the first and most important thing I had to do, was to put myself in the mix. Effectively, to commit to putting myself on the start line. If I did that, everything else could, or hopefully *would* follow. This, I came to realise, is the main difference between the people who do, and the people who don't. Not just with regard to the MDS, but anything and everything in life. The people who do are not necessarily more capable than the people who don't. More often the main difference is just that they are willing to give it a go. And just as importantly, willing to fail. So I mentally signed up.

I continued with my running. Nothing particularly arduous, but a half-marathon about every 6 weeks or so, and steady running on my own in between. My thoughts would return to the MDS in idle moments though. It had a strangely magnetic, alluring quality. I'd find myself daydreaming in the middle of the day, imagining what it would be like to experience the challenge for myself. I had been well and truly bitten by the MDS bug.

CHAPTER 3

Failure

Failure has never scared me; never even worried me. To be honest, it's never even really entered my thought process. What does it matter if you 'fail?' What does 'fail' even mean?

The Oxford English Dictionary defines 'failure' as thus:

Failure (n): the fact of someone or something not succeeding

So if you don't succeed, you automatically fail. It's a binary process. You haven't succeeded therefore you have automatically failed. I don't buy into this at all. At least not in totality. For me, "fail" should be redefined to mean something like 'trying to push the boundaries' or 'willing to give it a try.' And it's a completely internal, acutely personal judgment. I don't get to decide whether you've failed at something, and you certainly don't get to decide whether I have.

The minute you can internalize it and realise that the only person whose judgment matters is your own, you'll suddenly feel confident to take on challenges that you may have previously found intimidating. I know many, many people who would rather never try, so as to never fail. They're trapped in a vanilla mediocrity. I'm not criticizing it (much) but for me, that approach just doesn't work. I need the light and the shade, the peaks and the troughs.

As a kid, I would always rather try to jump over the stream and end up landing with wet feet, than spend the rest of the day wondering whether I could have made the jump. If you fail, the only people who would be happy are the people who wouldn't have the guts to do it themselves anyway. The threat of failure is to be embraced, not feared. If you never fail, you've probably never challenged yourself enough. After all, failure is the privilege of the few who have the guts to take the challenge on in the first place. The idea of sitting on a couch with safe boundaries around me scares me to death. Thinking I may never fail scares me just as much as thinking I may never succeed.

Consider the diagram below. You have two axes; one being the achieving of your objectives, and the second being happiness with your performance.

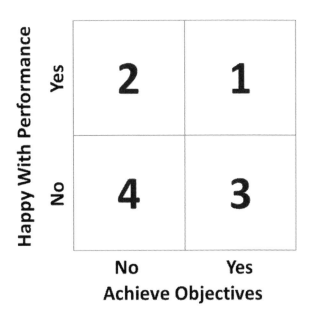

Clearly quadrant 1 is where we all want to be. Achieving our goals, and happy with our performance, and quadrant 4, the inverse of that, is where none of us want to be. But if you had to choose between quadrants 2 and 3, which would you go for? For me, it would be number 2 every single time. I've sat in all 4 quadrants many, many times, and know that for me the rank order of preference is as numbered in the diagram. If you're in quadrant 4, at least you get to say 'oh well, I messed that up, I'll have to go again.' If you're in quadrant 3 you're left with a slightly hollow feeling, thinking 'were my objectives challenging enough?' For me, that doesn't sit well at all.

I achieved B's at A-level. Not a bad result, and these grades got me entry into my first-choice university. Initially, I was over-the-moon. Then, in time, my school let me know my actual marks for my different subjects, and I found out that in each subject, I'd been extremely close, to achieving 'As,' only narrowly missing out by the smallest of margins. I was instantly crestfallen. My problem had been that I had never seen myself as an 'A Grade Student' so placed my expectations, and dare I say it, efforts, around achieving solid 'Bs.' Simply put, my expectations of myself weren't high enough. Sure, I technically 'succeeded' in that I achieved the grades I needed to get into my university of choice, but on hearing how close I'd been to A-grades, I instantly went from quadrant 1 to 3. It wasn't a pleasant place to be, and still mildly annoys me to this day. A-levels are meant to be an instantly understood and recognizable grade of success/achievement, but even they don't really work for me, because the truest judgment can only ever really come from within yourself.

What this means is we're free to set our goals and ambitions as high as possible, and we certainly shouldn't limit ourselves with what other people think they themselves are capable of. If we hit the goal, great, but if we don't, so what? As long as you're happy with how you performed, that is success in itself.

CHAPTER 4

I signed up to the MDS approximately 2 years in advance of the event itself. Paranoid about the places selling out and missing out on a slot, I sat with my laptop open and bank card ready, awaiting the countdown to the entry opening. As it transpired, I needn't have worried, because I registered a place without any issue at all (I went on to learn whilst in the Sahara that others had gained a place over a year after me). The confirmation email came in from Run Ultra, who are the UK agents for the MDS, and I was elated. I was in! This elation then very quickly turned into panic. What the fuck had I just done? What made me think I was remotely capable of taking on the MDS? How unbelievably arrogant could I possibly be?! I calmed myself down and read the confirmation email. It strongly recommended you take out insurance straight away, in case for any reason you were unable to participate in the event. I instantly decided against this. It struck me, from conversations I'd had, that a lot of people use the insurance as something of a comfort blanket, and it prevents them from fully committing to the event mentally. Some people definitely got cold feet in the run up to the event, spoke with a 'friendly' doctor, got a sick note, invoked their insurance and pretended none of it ever happened. I wasn't willing to risk being tempted to take this way out so ignored what was no doubt very sound advice.

If step one was signing up, and step two was ignoring any insurance, then step three in committing to the event was to shout my entry from the rooftops. I got myself onto twitter & Facebook, and shared news that I had gained entry into the MDS 2018. Sure, some of it was showing off and some of it was attention seeking, but mainly, it was further committing to the event. If no-one knew I was doing it, it would be very easy to silently withdraw my place and pretend it never happened. If, however, everyone knew my intentions, I'd look a bit of a fool if I then went on to withdraw. It was all designed to dial up maximum pressure on myself to succeed. I dare say an amateur psychologist would analyse my behaviour and suggest I was worried I wasn't going to deliver on my promise to myself. And this analysis would be right. I was petrified I wasn't up to the task, and needed any crutch I could lay hand to. Backed into a corner, and with all my friends knowing my intentions, I had to perform. It was the social media ultra-running equivalent of Babe Ruth calling his home run shot.

In the spirit of drawing on all possible sources of support, I began reading. I searched the Kindle store for 'Marathon Des Sables' and downloaded any titles that the search threw up. I read them all avidly, throughout the following 2-3 month period. The books I read were a range of 'couch to MDS' type books, to full on technical analysis manuals. I hadn't started specific training by this stage, and wanted to prepare myself as best I can. I figured I would be able to learn from other people's mistakes. The truth is though, after a few months reading, I was worn out emotionally, and told myself I had to stop the

MDS from becoming all-consuming. I ditched the books and just concentrated on running. Nothing too heavy, with a focus on enjoyment and time on feet. I told myself that I'd build up a bit of a mental plan for an official preparation plan that would kick in 12 months ahead of the race start. I got myself into decent shape and ran a half marathon in 1hr20m. I'd actually treated the race as a training run, and didn't go 'all out' and fancied I could have dipped below the 1hr20m if I'd pushed it a bit harder. (That I didn't still rankles with me as this 1hr20m remains my half-marathon PB and I'd so much rather it be beneath that threshold!)

Unfortunately, fast forwarding a touch, it was precisely at T-minus 12 months that life became very busy, and very stressful. The forklift business became extremely intense and stressful. The recent vote out of the EU meant that our customers all of a sudden became very unpredictable in their behaviour. Regrettably, I'm not one of those people who can use exercise as a means of de-stressing. The only way I can de-stress is to focus time on the matter that is causing the stress, and this meant more time in the office. One day, I tried to leave the office early to do a 20 mile run. I got 5 miles into it and had to stop. I just couldn't concentrate – feeling guilty for not being at my desk, working. I started to think the unthinkable... I may have to pull out of the race. I mentioned this to Lucy, who offered up some fairly tough love, and told me to keep plugging away. I did just that, and told myself to stop being so dramatic

By pure chance, around this time, I was approached by another business who wanted to purchase our business. The details aren't relevant for here, but after a series of meetings and a period of negotiation, we decided to make the extremely difficult decision to part with what had been a family business of very nearly 40 years. I had literally never known family life without the business, and the approach had come entirely out of the blue. I had taken a lot of time to consider our options and whilst an intensely emotional decision, I knew that it was the right thing to do.

A coincidental, yet happy by-product of the decision was a lot less stress, and a lot more time. In the Autumn of 2017, I put together a plan of attack for the MDS. **My MDS.**

My plan wasn't super scientific, but I felt comfort in just having a plan, of sorts:

- I would up my mileage to c50 miles per week until Christmas (that my mileage was below 50 miles per week gives an idea of how I'd be struggling for time up until this point)
- I would clean my diet up
- Post-Christmas I would up my mileage steadily, to culminate in a 100 mile week around 6 weeks before departure
- I would start running with weight in the new year
- I would look to toughen my feet immediately
- I would enter both the Druids and Pilgrims Ultras
- I would try to source myself some 'tent buddies' before departure
- And ultimately, I would stop worrying about it, start enjoying it, and take control of the situation. This was MY race. I had entered it. I would decide what I wanted out of it, and this would dictate how I approached it.

Kit details and nutrition, I mentally put on another to-do list.

CHAPTER 5

Before long, it was early November, and time for the Druids multi-day ultra-marathon. I was both excited and nervous about this event. It was my first multi-day ultra, and it wasn't for the faint at heart. The event was 3 days long, and totaled 84 miles. Having not really done any overt 'speed work' in over a year, I was a long way short of my previous marathon and half marathon times. This wasn't important to me though. It was all about time on feet, and stepping stones towards the big sandy adventure.

Being a little nervous, and more than a little bit anti-social at times, I took the option of booking a hotel for the evenings, rather than sleeping on the floor in a school hall which was the de-facto arrangement if you didn't make other plans. I spoke with the event organiser, and they recommended a specific hotel and said they would arrange transport for me and other competitors.

On the first morning we were transported out to the start line which was up on the Ridgeway in Buckinghamshire. It was extremely exposed and very, very windy. The organiser took a photo of us all on the start line and set us on our way. There was an awful lot of chat about the MDS and I quickly found most of it rather irritating. Everyone seemed to be an expert, and everyone seemed to know more than the next man. It reminded me of waiting to go into the exam hall for my A-Levels. All the other 6th formers would be confidently droning on about how many hours revision they had done, and how they were confident they could predict this year's Macro-Economic essay question as they had studied every past paper dating back to Edwardian times. I would stand there thinking, *'I doubt you've done as much revision as you're claiming, but I can also, quite confidently state that you've done more than me. Because I've done pretty much fuck all.'* It really was like that though. I overheard one chap saying to another 'you're only at 80 miles a week? Wow, you're really going to struggle.' I muttered 'prick' to myself and decided to put my earphones in and blank it all out.

At Druids, they have fueling stops where they offer up delights such as sausage rolls, pretzels, jelly babies and sandwiches. This is great because, if you're not too fussy, you can get away with just taking fluids with you. This was what I did; taking a camelback with electrolyte tablets along with some energy gels. I really enjoyed the first day, and completed the 29.3 mile mainly trail based course in 5hr21 minutes, finishing 44th out of 147. I was really happy with how it had gone, and crucially, had held a lot back for the subsequent days.

When I got back into the event tent at the end of the first day, I spoke with an organiser and reminded them of their offer to transport me to my hotel. 'Yeah, no problem buddy,' came the cheerful response. Things turned a bit awkward though when they asked me which hotel I was in. When I told them, the chap replied 'what the hell are you staying there for? It's miles away!' I said that they had recommended it! It turned out there had been an admin error and they had told me the wrong hotel, but that they would transport me as promised.

I returned to my hotel, had a bath, got some food on board and set my alarm for the morning. The chap who dropped me off said he would pick me up at 8am. All was well with the world. I settled into my bed, content in the knowledge that I could be sleeping on a floor down the road. I'd set my alarm for 7am, to allow myself an hour to eat and decide on what kit to wear once I'd had a chance to check the weather. I slept like a baby and was duly woken at 7am by my alarm. All hell broke loose quite literally 10 seconds later, however, when my phone rang. It was the chap who was due to pick me up. He said he was outside. I was barely awake and confused. I told him I thought he was coming in an hour. He said, 'yeah, well we decided you could go on the earlier start, so I'm here now. Can you get down here asap?' The sensible thing would have been to say 'no, I'm not ready, you'll have to wait and I'll see you in a bit.' As it was, I said 'oh, ok, I'll be down as soon as I can.' I threw on some kit without even opening the curtains, and ran downstairs.

Once in the car, travelling to the start, I began to realise I'd made a pretty fundamental error, kit-wise. It was fairly chilly and drizzling. I was wearing some shorts and a t-shirt style top. This wasn't going to be enough. But my inexperience and overall naivety of the situation meant I didn't do anything about it. Nor did I do anything about the fact that I hadn't had any breakfast; literally nothing at all. Fortunately I had filled up my camelback the night before so I had that with me, fully loaded. As we approached the carpark that was doubling up as the start line, I saw the other competitors gathered for the briefing. The man driving said 'you'll have to get a wriggle on son,' so I dashed out of the car and joined the others. As I stood there, I realised I was very cold, but told myself it would be ok once I started running.

Soon enough, they set us off, and I did indeed warm up. I felt pretty good actually, and enjoyed myself no end. I knew that I'd not eaten anything, so knew I needed to deal with it. I set off slowly. The thing with an ultra, or even a marathon, is that if you're not careful, you can write cheques in the early miles, that your body's not going to be able to cash towards the end of the race. I knew I needed to keep a lot in reserve, and I knew I needed to get some food on board. I ate as much as I could at the first two check points, and felt that things were going ok. Around mile 19 however, I started to suffer. By this point, it was fairly cold, and I was wet through. I slowed to a walk and began shivering. I'd run out of fuel, and had basically hit the wall.

I was pretty sure that I could 'grin and bear it' and get through the remaining 10 miles. I was wrong. I got colder and colder, and eventually resorted to getting my tinfoil blanket out of my backpack to try to keep warm. The final check point was at mile 25ish, and I knew I could get there. Runners were over-taking me and every one of them sounded concerned. I realised I must look pretty bad. After an eternity, I saw the checkpoint in the distance. Then I saw a course official jogging down the pathway to meet me. He got to me and said that some other competitors had said there was someone struggling. I was pissed off. I didn't like that I'd been newsworthy for all the wrong reasons. The official was very calm and comforting though. He walked with me to the checkpoint and told me to get in a car that was there.

In the car, he gave me a cup of tea, and put all the heaters on me. I thought I'd get myself warm, and get going in a few minutes, but 20 minutes later, I still couldn't get warm. Eventually, he said that they wouldn't let me continue as they felt I probably had the early stages of hypothermia. I was now even more pissed off. It was less than 3 miles to the finish, and I was sure I could get there without any significant danger. As cheesed off as I was though, I'm not thick enough to not see when someone's looking out for my health, so licked my wounds and tried to make pleasant conversation with the gent as he drove me back.

On return to the race center, I was given hot soup, chocolate and a blanket. Within an hour or so my temperature was back up and they 'released me.' I was out of the race though, so got a lift back to the hotel. I phoned Lucy and explained I'd be back earlier than planned. Whilst I was desperately disappointed to be out of the race, I tried to take comfort in the knowledge that this was the furthest I had ever run in a two day period. I got home, cracked open a bottle of wine (probably not the best post-ultra refueling ever, but I had to find a silver lining somewhere!) and settled down for the evening. The next day, I got up and ran 15 miles around the lanes near home. All in all, it wasn't a total disaster. I'd run further than I ever had before, in a 3-day period, despite considerable elements that were far from ideal.

CHAPTER 6

Come the new year, my preparations increased in intensity. I decided I wanted / needed to shift a stone in weight, so cleaned up my food. Within 4 weeks, I'd dropped that stone, and started to feel in pretty good condition. I had signed up to the Pilgrims 2 day Ultra that was organised by the same people who organise Druids. This event was in early February, and was going to be frequented by most UK based people who were entered into the MDS. I elected to stay in the school gym in a bid to meet people, and hopefully stumble upon some potential tent buddies.

The Pilgrims course is basically a 33 mile per day, 'out & back' along some very muddy trails, with the odd bit of road thrown in here and there. It's a tough, tough course, and was made tougher by the presence of the thickest mud I'd ever run in. The elevation is also very challenging. The race takes in Box Hill on the North Downs, which was used as part of the cycling route at the 2012 Olympics. That said, I had a really good first day, again remembering to hold something back for day 2, finishing in 36th place out of 244 people, in 5hrs45mins. Along the way, I had got chatting to a guy who I would ultimately share a tent with in the desert. Paul was historically more of a cyclist than a runner, but had done an Ironman, and that merited serious respect in my book. He hadn't actually entered the Pilgrims race but was running part of the route as it went near his home. We agreed to keep in touch in the run up to the desert.

The over-night stay in the school hall was interesting. They laid on food and put a TV on to show the 6 Nations rugby, which made me extremely happy. There were also two speakers organised. The first was Neil Thubron who is the main guy at XNRG. I didn't know much about him before, but he spoke extremely eloquently about the common characteristics amongst people who succeed in events such as the MDS. The one that stood out to me was when he said 'it has to matter. It has to mean something. And if it means something to people other than just you, there is an increased chance you will succeed. We will work harder for others than we will do for ourselves.' This resonated with me at a very personal level, and chimed with one of my core motivations for doing the race.

Every night, since they had been born, when I kissed my kids goodnight, I would say to them 'Remember! You can be anyone you want to be, and you can achieve anything you want to achieve, because daddy loves you!' I really wanted (and still want!) to instill a sense of confidence in our kids; a sense of being confident to give things a try, and of not being fearful of failure. I had long figured that one of the best ways of taking this message beyond just words, was by trying to prove it to them. I wanted to try to do something that I wasn't sure I could achieve, in a bid to proving to them that they could have the confidence to take on challenges that may seem, at first glance, beyond their reach. So what Neil said made perfect sense. I would channel that sense of it mattering to Millie and Ted.

The second speaker was the legendary ultra-runner, Elisabet Barnes. Elisabet had won the MDS previously, and is extremely well known and respected on the circuit. She explained that , that day – the first day of Pilgrims, we had run further than we would on any of the days in the desert, other than the long day. She then explained that by the close of the next day, we would have completed 25% further than the long stage of the MDS, in a shorter time frame than the time limit on that stage when out in Morocco. The other salient point that she made was that all the statistics show that you are far more likely to pull out of the MDS before getting to the start line, rather than out on the course itself. The key was getting to the start line in good shape. Her talk was obviously designed to build confidence, and it did a job. I still sat there plagued with self-doubt though. Could I really do it? I looked around the room at the other people who had indicated they, too, were signed up for the MDS and told myself, if they could do it, I could do it. It was now just the small matter of finishing the return leg on Day 2.

One thing had to happen first, however. I had to sleep on the floor, in a school gym, on the mat I was planning on taking to the desert. It was torture! It was so unbelievably uncomfortable that I barely slept a wink. (It didn't help that there was a chorus of snoring, rustling, farting, coughing and sneezing throughout the night). I got up in the morning as stiff as a board. This was going to be a hard day! I had a good breakfast of some of the food I was planning on taking to the desert (more on nutrition later), stretched off as best I could, and headed to the start line along with everyone else. They got us underway and I was alarmed at how bad I felt. I was so incredibly stiff! After a few miles though, I started to ease up and began to move more freely.

After an hour or so, we approached a steep descent. The previous day, this had been an extremely tough section, with steps cut into the mud of the hillside. Unfortunately, I found it just as tough going down the steps, as I had going up them less than 24 hours before. It wasn't so much fitness that was my issue, but a lack of technical ability. Some people were able to skip down them at high speed, whilst I was constantly struggling for decent purchase underfoot. Whilst frustrating, I saw the whole event as very much a training run, so didn't think about it too much and pushed on ahead.

The thing with these races is that you very often 'cat & mouse' specific people throughout the course. This started to happen on Day 2 of Pilgrims. People would overtake me on downhill sections and I'd then reel them in on the flats and uphill bits. It was good to chat to them as they went past me, or vice-versa. It seemed like everyone there would be on the plane to Morocco in April, and it made me feel more relaxed knowing I was in their company.

Eventually, I approached the final mile or so of the course. My target had been to finish in the same time as I'd completed the first day, but my inability to deal with the downhill sections had ensured this very quickly became unattainable. I set my target as finishing within one hour of my time on Day 1, and achieved it to the minute. My finishing time was 6hr45mins, placing me 70th out of 212. I was over the moon! Before the event, and following my DNF at Druids, I had mentally set this as a key target. I felt that if I could complete Pilgrims in a reasonably competitive manner, I would stand a chance in the desert. The final few miles of Day 2 at Pilgrims had been extremely tough going, and I had been forced to dig very deep mentally. I felt far more confident having successfully completed the race, and took a picture of the medal being put over my head, in a bid to further bolster my confidence.

CHAPTER 7

By mid-February, the MDS had taken over my life completely. Via Paul, who I had met running Pilgrims, I had managed to bag myself a tent load of friendly faces (or, more accurately, 'friendly whatsappers' as I hadn't actually met any of them). My thoughts were never far away from the MDS with the event creeping into my head regularly, even when I was trying to concentrate on other things. I was aware that I was becoming increasingly difficult to live with. I was generally quite irritable and short of patience, mainly through stress and worry.

The main mental problem I had with the MDS was that no matter how much training I did, I worried that I wasn't doing enough. Training for a marathon is pretty easy. Realistically, your week is going to feature a speed session, a tempo run, and a long run. You know what you've got to do, and the seemingly infinite resources out there will give you confidence in the plan you are following. Despite the legendary, and fairly famous nature of the MDS though, there is actually precious little by means of readily available training programmes. Couple this with the fact that the MDS is designed to push you to the absolute brink of your physical and mental capabilities, and no matter what run I went on, I'd get in the shower afterwards and think 'maybe I should have done an extra 5 miles,' or 'was that really enough time on my feet?' I had to keep back-referencing Pilgrims to convince myself all was well. I'd finished 38th out of a field of around 220 (it's difficult to know the exact number due to some people running one day and not the other, and a fair few people dropping out). This became a constant frame of reference; 'remember Pilgrims.... Remember Pilgrims....'

I took a trip down to MyRaceKit in Southend on Sea. MyRaceKit is owned by the aforementioned Elisabet Barnes and a one-stop-shop for all of your MDS requirements. A few hours with them kitted me out with all I required (full kit list in appendix) whilst also relieving me of a not inconsiderable quantity of money. With my kit sorted, it really felt like the MDS was within touching distance. I then became, quite predictably, obsessed with my pack weight. I really wanted my pack to come in under 8kg, which would mean that with 1.5 litres of water, I'd be weighing in at 9.5kg with full bottles. This was crucial to achieving a calm state of mind. I'd owned a 10kg weight vest for years, and had done lots of running with it on, so coming in under that was a real boost mentally. And trust me, the difference between 8kg and 10kg is considerable when you're running marathons! The only problem was, when I weighed all of my kit, it was coming in at 10kg, excluding water. I reviewed things....

Some people are militant in their pursuit of weight-saving. They research and purchase the lightest possible mandatory items and take only these mandatories, and food. Others are prepared to carry a little more weight if it equates to greater comfort when not racing. My approach was somewhere between the two. I would take the mandatories plus:

- My Garmin Forerunner 235 GPS watch (and associated charger cable). It was essential to me that I could track my progress, so this was non-negotiable. The charger cable was equally essential.
- My iPhone. I wanted to have the option of music whilst out there, and also have the ability to document the event with a camera. My phone was the obvious solution.
- 2 pairs of the lightest weight headphones I could find.
- Flip flops. This was a matter of quite some debate. Some people suggested flip flops were unnecessary, and you could wear your running shoes without the insoles, of an evening. (The idea being that removing the insoles increased the room available for your likely swollen feet.) Others strongly advised that being able to allow your feet to breathe after hours cooped up in your socks, shoes and gaiters, was a big positive. I decided to go with the flip flops, on the basis that I would ditch them if I didn't need them.
- A buff. They don't weigh much, and I thought would be useful in sandstorms, the cold, the heat, and any other time really!
- A 'stove' and pot for heating my food. In reality, the stove is tiny, and the pot was pretty much an essential, it seemed.
- Some fuel for heating my food. In the event, I actually ditched this fuel in order to save weight, and instead collected scrub and wood from around the camp, and burned this instead.
- A charging block to charge both my watch and my phone.
- Some cable ties. For emergencies.
- 2 spare laces. Again, for emergencies.

I then decanted all of my food into labelled up freezer bags, in order to save weight. It saved a surprising amount – 450g, which was a right result, and meant that all in my pack was coming in at bang on 8kg. Perfect.

The weekend I carried out my 'decanting' was the weekend I would normally be on a ski trip with all my closest buddies who I used to play rugby with. This year, I had taken the very easy, yet very difficult decision to not go. Going would have been ridiculous. It's an extremely boozy trip and carries with it the standard dangers of injury whilst skiing. I would never have forgiven myself if I'd gone and hurt myself. That said, I was gutted when all the whatsapp messages started flooding through, telling me just what an amazing time they were having without me. I tried to leave the group chat but they added me back in! On the Saturday night, they sent me the kind of torrid abuse that is saved only for close friends, telling me what a loser I was, along with photos of themselves resembling the camera reel at the end of The Hangover. I sent back a photo of my scales showing a 450g weight saving following my change in packaging saying 'you may be having the time of your lives, but I've just saved 450g by replacing my foil packaging with lightweight sandwich bags. Who's the loser now?!'

Whilst joking, I was extremely disappointed to be missing out on what was one of my favourite weekends of the year. The sacrifice was entirely appropriate however. It strengthened my resolve and meant that I had another thing to look back on whilst out in the desert, as a means to motivate myself, drive myself forward, and refuse to give up.

CHAPTER 8

Nutrition

I've dedicated a whole chapter to nutrition and am dreading writing it to be honest. The reason being, I find it really boring. But I'm hoping my experience and learning may help save other people time. Given my admission for turning up for exams having done minimal revision, it probably comes as no surprise when I say I'd developed a bit of a habit of 'winging it' when it came to nutrition and races. As I type this, I am aware of how ridiculous it sounds, but I love running, not the admin that precedes it, so I'd typically neglected it through lack of interest. That said, the times that I had got it right, I **always** felt the benefit. I was determined, therefore, to get it absolutely perfect for such an extreme challenge.

Most runners will have experienced 'runger.' The day after a long run, I would typically eat the house. I would stuff down a ridiculous quantity of food. This really concerned me. I was going to be doing a 'long run' each day for a week, so presumably, I'd want to stuff myself every single day?! As silly as it sounds, this prospect concerned me a lot. I was extremely worried that I wouldn't be able to take enough calories with me, and would end up running out of fuel, just as I had on day 2 of Druids. Eventually, the only way I could convince myself that it would be ok, was to tell myself that there were hundreds of other people doing it, in the exact same boat, so presumably it must be possible. To be honest, this became my default fall-back position for most issues that concerned me!

The MDS rules state that each competitor must have a minimum of 14,000 calories on board at the start of the race. This equates to 2,000 calories per day, and you must always have a minimum of 2,000 calories for each day of the race remaining. This may be checked by officials throughout the race. I had bonked on a number of occasions in races, and also run out of fuel on long training runs, so decided that 2,000 calories wouldn't be enough for me. My racing weight would be around 12 stones, which would be a little heavier than the quicker runners who were able to survive on less. I felt that around 2,500 calories per day would be prudent for me.

I quickly started researching which foods offered maximum calorific content for minimum weight. Macadamia nuts were a clear favourite here, and featured highly on the Facebook forum. Beyond this, I decided to go with freeze dried meals. I tried various options out there and decided upon an assortment from Expedition Foods. They were palatable enough, and contained the calories I needed. My general approach was for each day to contain:
- A high calorie breakfast

- Some snacks for out on the course
- A recovery shake
- A high calorie dinner
- An energy bar

This was flexed slightly around both the long day, and also the final 10k day, where I made the calories up solely with macadamia nuts.

My full nutrition list is set out below:

Day 1 31k		Weight (g)	Calories
Breakfast	Granola breakfast	240	1000
Snacks	Macadamia nuts	100	718
Drink	Tribe recovery shake raspberry	20	160
Meal	Chilli with rice	155	800
Snacks	Grenade bar	60	218
			2,896
Day 2 39k			
Breakfast	Porridge with sultanas	180	800
Snacks	Dried mango	100	328
Drink	Tribe recovery shake Vanilla	20	156
Meal	Beef stroganoff and rice	135	800
Snacks	Grenade Bar	60	218
			2,302
Day 3 32k			
Breakfast	Porridge with blueberries	180	800
Snacks	Chilli beef	69	146

Snacks	Macadamia nuts	100	718
Drink	Tribe recovery shake cocoa	20	157
Meal	Asian noodles with beef	165	800
Snacks	Grenade bar	60	218
			2,839
Day 4 86k			
Breakfast	Granola breakfast	240	1000
Snacks	Fruit and nut mix	100	408
Snacks	Macadamia nuts	100	718
Load shake	Strawberry & Vanilla	69	270
Snacks	Dried mango	100	328
Drink	Tribe recovery shake Vanilla	20	156
Snacks	Peperami	60	102
Snacks	Chilli beef	69	146
			3,128
Day 5 (continuation from Day 4)			
Meal	Beef stroganoff and rice	135	800
Snacks	Macadamia nuts	100	718
Snacks	Grenade Bar	60	218
Meal	Beef and potato hotpot	148	800
			2,536
Day 6 42k			
Breakfast	Porridge with Strawberries	165	800
Snacks	9 superseed bar	50	227
Snacks	9 superseed bar	50	227
Snacks	Dried mango	100	328
Drink	Tribe recovery shake	20	160

	raspberry		
Meal	Spaghetti Bolognese	160	800
			2,542
Day 7 8k			
Breakfast	Macadamia nuts	250	1795
Snacks	Grenade Bar	60	218
			2013
	Total	**3,720g**	**18,256**

In addition, I included a collection of peanut M&Ms and Haribo, that I put in 7 'money bags.' I thought they would be a nice 'treat' to look forward to each evening, but did not include them in my calorie count. I also included 14x energy gels and 14x electrolyte tablets.

Overall, I think I got my nutrition just about spot on. In terms of both quantity and variety, I was very happy with what I had taken. There was a lot of information detailing how 'your tastes change when in the desert.' They may do, but to be honest, I didn't really notice. More of that later!

What was key to success, was preparation. Eating all of the meals beforehand to check that I could stomach them, and crucially that I could run on them. It may seem obvious, but lots of people didn't perform this check. It seemed ludicrous to me. I mean, I love curry, but I know I can't run on it! It was essential to my sense of calm and preparation that I knew I could run on whatever fuel I was planning on putting into my pack. It was also important to check I could cook it on the 'stove' I was taking. 'Stove' is a bit of an exaggeration really. The popular item is a metal contraption that works like an inverted tripod. It has a small area for you to put fuel tablets, and your pot sits on the three prongs, with the burning underneath heating your water. This worked fine, so I knew I was fully prepared.

CHAPTER 9

The back end of February was when my training really kicked up a gear. I had set myself a goal of running a 100 mile week. It had long been in the plan, and was a bit of a mental comfort blanket. I'm not sure why 100 miles would make me feel so much better than 99 miles, but it definitely would! I reasoned that it was only a little over a half marathon a day, so would be easily achievable. Unfortunately, the week I had earmarked for it coincided with an extremely cold spell. The temperature was well below freezing most days, with the roads and pavements covered in ice. I did the best I could, and did a fair bit on the treadmill, which was pretty soul destroying. I finished up with 96 miles for the week, having run out of time due to a couple of work commitments. It didn't bother me; mainly because I knew the additional 4 miles could have been achieved physically, without any problem whatsoever. Yes, it was a shame that I hadn't hit the magic 100 number, but it was the furthest I had ever run in a week, and I felt absolutely fine. Things were coming together nicely.

The onset of March brought things into close focus. I was doing the MDS 'next month!' All of my focus now was on not getting injured, and fine tuning my feet and body to ensure the best possible preparation. I had been applying Gehwol cream to my feet to toughen up the skin and hopefully prevent blisters. I redoubled my efforts here which was a bit of a pain as it took time for the cream to soak into my feet, before I could put socks on. Just one more life disruption courtesy of the MDS! I packed and repacked my bag and ran with it on every other run. I could maybe have run with my pack more often, but I was very focused on not picking up any injuries.

It was around this time that my fundraising really took off. I had chosen to raise money for the Community First Responder organisation who had attended to my dad when he had his heart-attack. They hadn't been able to save him, but their work is so valuable within the rural communities, and they are entirely funded via donations. Having a 'cause' helped with the training. It was motivating to know that I was actually achieving something tangible for such a worthy cause. I relied totally on social media to get my message out, and now I was able to state that within a few weeks I would be on the start line, the donations started coming in thick and fast. I finished up raising over £7,500 for the charity, which was far higher than I could have ever dreamt.

The other thing that happened around this time, was I took out insurance. I hadn't previously taken any insurance out as I didn't want any form of safety net that may have encouraged me to not make it to the start line. I read of insurance policies that would reimburse you if you were insured and couldn't race. As I have said, I had a theory that some people would enter the race, take the insurance and then find the training quite tough. They could speak with a friendly doctor and request a medical note, that they could then use to reclaim the cost of their entry, should they wish to pull out. I didn't want this option. I was fully committed; I hadn't wanted to give myself a get out of jail free card. The rules stipulate however, that you need to have an ECG heart-trace done, for them to allow you on the start line. Given my dad had died of a heart-attack, I figured there was a chance the ECG could throw up something that would prevent me from running.

For your ECG to be valid, it has to have been conducted within 4 weeks of the race start. I spoke with my GP and they didn't want to know. I didn't get much beyond the receptionist so started looking into other options. At this point, Rory Coleman announced that his brother was a GP and would hold a clinic in London for anyone who wanted to come along. Perfect! I booked myself a slot, and the night before signed up for the insurance in case the ECG threw up a problem.

Unlike most other areas, I did very little research into the insurance on offer. A quick scan of the social media forums suggested that Dog Tag was the firm to go with, so I paid my money (yet more money!) and completed the penultimate part of the jigsaw. I can't really expand on the detail of my insurance cover as I didn't pay a lot of attention, which looking back, was a little stupid.

The next day, I jumped on a train down to London and arrived at the building that was being used by Rory and his brother. It was quite surreal meeting Rory. He's a legend within the ultra-running community, but is also something of a marmite character (no offence, Rory). He is one of the most experienced ultra-runners in the world, and isn't shy on offering his opinion. I'd been warned to not take everything he says as gospel. It is, after all, just one man's opinion. Yet it is also the opinion of an extremely experienced man! I went into it with an open mind, and really enjoyed the relatively short time I spent with him. It turned out he grew up not far from me and we had quite a few shared friends. As I sat waiting to see his brother however, I started to experience the familiar feeling of butterflies in my stomach, and a dry mouth. Blimey I was nervous! The man I was about to see was going to decide whether I could step on the start line or not. Should I mention my dad's heart attack to him, to explain away any issues he may see? Or should I definitely not mention it? I decided to definitely not mention it!

Rory's brother told me to lie down and put the sensors on me. I could feel my heart going like the clappers and what felt like my blood pressure going through the roof. *Jesus fucking Christ, this wasn't in the plan.* Let alone pass the test, I would be lucky to not make it out of there on a stretcher at this rate. He was evidently used to this though, and was very good at trying to put me at ease. But this was it. This was everything in one moment. The hundreds, and hundreds of miles in training. The sacrifices we had made as a family. The money I had been sponsored! It may all have been about to be rendered worthless and a waste of time. But then far sooner than I was expecting, he said, *'great, you're good to go. Slight 'runner's heart' but I've seen nothing there that suggests you shouldn't be on the start line.'* And just like that, it was over. I was actually quite taken aback, and a little lost for words. I felt I needed to thank him; to show my gratitude. But what had he actually done? He'd merely carried out a test, that I had passed. What was I thanking him for?! But I did thank him. Repeatedly. Before hot-footing it out of the room before he had a chance to change his mind.

As I settled back into my seat on the train, I had a little smile to myself. It was on. And as we would say down my rugby club, it was on like Donkey Kong! I was doing it. The final piece of the puzzle had been put in place. Nothing was going to stop me now. This prompted a combination of huge excitement, and also, a sense of fear. If I'm brutally honest, a failed ECG could have been the ultimate in gallant failure. Unable to make it to the start line, and therefore put myself through hell, due to a technicality not of my doing. Now I'm not saying I wanted that at all, but passing the test, which I had so desperately wanted to do, had removed this as an option. Speaking to people when I was out in the desert, I know that I wasn't the only one to have experienced this strange, fleeting contradiction in emotions. I put my headphones in, and started listening to the playlist I was creating for my time on the course, and remembered the bi-product information I had been given; my heart was in good working order. Given what had happened to my dad, this was extremely good news. Yet in the scheme of the MDS it seemed relatively insignificant. It was ON!

Your ECG is a critical part of your kit for the MDS. Without it they will not allow you on the start line, so I pinned it to the noticeboard with a large 'DO NOT THROW IN BIN' stuck on it.

Around this time, I started trying to gradually acclimatise myself to the heat that was to come. I messaged a load of friends and managed to borrow 6 heaters that I used to surround my treadmill at home. I would turn them all on full for half an hour before I ran, and close the door on the room. This enabled me to get the room temperature up around 42c according to my thermometer, although I'm not sure how accurate an 'air temperature' it provided. I put extra layers on, two hats, and a fully laden back pack and would run for an hour or so at a time. I did this 3 times a week for the month running up to my departure. It was extremely uncomfortable, and the sweat would pour off me. Lucy would walk past the glass door to the 'running room' and shake her head with a rueful smile. Psychologically though, it felt like I was getting ahead of the game a touch. Whilst I couldn't logistically go warm-weather training, this was the next best thing. I remember looking at the reflection of myself in the glass door, as I pounded away at the treadmill and thinking to myself 'is that a man who can run across a desert?' It wouldn't be long until I found out.

CHAPTER 10

The week before departure saw my emotions and stress levels settle down a touch. The penultimate week prior to departure, I had been extremely tense; worrying about a variety of things that I had already boxed off, but forgotten about. Now, with less than 7 days to go, I was willing the departure to come around as soon as possible. I'd prepared as best I could, and now I just wanted to get underway. I wanted all the chat, the thinking and the preparation to be over. More than anything else, I wanted to be in the desert.

Whilst my emotions *did* settle down, I became intensely paranoid about the state of my health. Given very little training was going on by this stage, there was little chance of getting injured. There was, however, every chance of becoming ill. Turning up on the start-line with a cold, a dodgy stomach, or even just mildly under the weather, could be catastrophic. I'm normally pretty relaxed about my health, however the paranoia became extremely real. If I was out and someone sneezed near me, I'd tut to myself, stare accusingly and sidle away. I found myself unconsciously not cuddling my kids as tightly (kids are germ factories after all!) I worked hard to be rational and overcome this paranoia however it had a mind of its own. A mate came round to see me and wish me luck, and arrived with a sniffle. Rather than feel grateful for his thoughtfulness in making the trip to wish me well, my acute mental state saw me bewildered as to why he'd do something so reckless as to potentially give me a cold. I really was on a knife edge emotionally.

I did have one further major last minute panic, and it was a very significant one. For a full 18 months, I had struggled to decide on a pair of shoes for the desert. I'd tried trail shoes, x-trail shoes and more rigid roadies, yet hadn't found a pair that had obviously stood out as being 'the ones.' I had been planning on taking a pair of Brooks Ghost, but hadn't actually found them to be perfect. I'd considered this to be understandable, given they were more rigid than my typical road shoes. I had wrestled with the shoe-choice conundrum for months, and must have driven them mad in my local sports shop. Then, the week before departure, I had a moment of clarity... I suddenly thought, 'if I'm taking road shoes, why don't I just take my favourite road shoes?!' So I nipped to my favourite local sports shop, bought a pair of Brooks Pure Cadence, and then considered how I was going to get some Velcro stitched to them in order to accommodate my gaiters. I nipped to a local haberdashery with my Ghosts that had already been tailored by the guys at MyRaceKit and showed the lady what I needed. She pulled out a roll of exactly what I was after, and I hurried off after giving her the £2.25 she requested (a pleasingly small amount given how expensive the MDS is!).

I took the trainers and Velcro to a local cobbler who shook his head and said he wouldn't do it. I started to panic a touch, but decided on a different tact with the second cobbler. 'A cobbler down in London did this for me,' I said, whilst showing him my Ghosts. 'He says that there's no cobbler outside London who can do this!' The chap peered at my shoes, and the strip of Velcro. 'Come back in a couple of hours,' he said. And that was that. 3 hours later, I had two pairs of Velcro'd up trainers, and I was ready to go.

It's important to state that before I departed for the desert, I ran in my new trainers for about 2 hours, in order to break them in. I also wore them for the travel to the desert, to further break them in. It would be absolute lunacy to attempt any race in brand new, untested shoes! In addition, I actually took both my Pure Cadence and Ghosts to the desert, in order to hedge my bets a touch, right up until the last minute.

For the remainder of the week, it was a case of hot baths, hot saunas, light running, and continuing to try not to get ill. Over the years, Lucy had learned how to handle me in the days before a 'big' event and backed off a touch. She knew that I had to process and reprocess things; not because I was unsure of detail, but because it served as a sort of therapy. I just needed to keep busy; to not have too much time to think.

With each bedtime that came and went, I became steadily calmer, whilst also feeling a sense of finality. Whilst I'd not yet left for the desert, we as a family had already been on a significant adventure in my preparations for the event. Millie wanted to talk about the race in detail, with her main focus on whether I would 'beat the camel.' *(At the MDS, you need to pass through checkpoints within specific cut-off times. A physical representation of these times is a camel that walks sweeps up the back of the field. Legend has it that if the camel overtakes you, you are retired from the race. This became a very easy concept for Millie to latch onto. "Daddy must beat the camel!")* Her excitement and interest was both touching and motivating. It reached the point however, that I didn't want to talk about it too much. I was worried that I may be setting myself up for a fall.

Soon enough, it was the night before my departure. Lucy and I chatted as we lay in bed. For the one and only time, she asked 'do you think you'll do it, Dunc?' I didn't really know what to say, so just told the truth. 'I hope so,' I said. 'Me too,' came her honest and simple reply. I lay in bed that night looking at the ceiling and wondered to myself whether the next time I looked at the ceiling I'd have a medal, or a DNF next to my name. Eventually I drifted off to sleep.

I woke up the next day and padded around the house without much purpose. I was fully packed and ready to go, so it was just a case of killing time really. My brother had offered to drive me down to the airport. This was good news. My brother is a very calm guy, and isn't someone to say something when nothing needs saying. When he offered up his services, I was really grateful as it meant that I could enjoy the last couple of hours before the MDS madness really kicked in, without too much emotion.

I gave my two kids a big hug and a kiss. Ted was too young, at 4, to really understand what was going on and how long I would be away for. Millie had a much better grasp of the situation. She'd been quite upset about me going away for what was not far off two weeks. The great news was that I was due to return the night before her 7th birthday. (When you book the MDS, you don't actually know the specific dates, and the way the race typically fell, there had been a good chance that I would have been away for her birthday. *Just one more example of how selfish I'd been prepared to be in order to pursue this dream.*) Millie was a little sad, but also knew enough to know that what I was off to do was, in her words, 'really difficult.' She kissed me goodbye and asked me if I would promise to bring her back a finisher's medal for her birthday. I took a rather emotional and deep gulp, and replied that 'yes I would.' I then made a similarly emotional goodbye to Lucy before jumping in the car to head off.

My brother hadn't even taken the handbrake off though, when I leapt back out of the car before returning 30 seconds later. 'What had you forgotten?' my brother asked. 'Panicked I didn't have enough bog roll!' I laughed. The drive down was uneventful, discussing anything but the event itself. Pretty quickly he was dropping me off at my hotel in the terminal at Gatwick. The receptionist looked at me with an amused smile. 'Not the first chap to come in here clutching a backpack, some trainers and a spare bog roll?' I asked. He chuckled and said 'You're about number 50.' Excellent. I was in the right place. I waved my brother off and nipped up to my room.

As I sat and checked my bag for the umpteenth time that day, I stumbled across two handwritten notes hidden in my towel. One from Lucy, and one from my daughter. The contents of the letters should remain private, but they both, for their individual reasons resonated with me more than anything else I'd ever read. What took me back was how they both understood what this meant, and *how much* this meant. That may sound glib. Surely your wife would understand? But people don't always understand your dreams, your motives and your goals. Particularly when you're not even sure you understand them yourself. They did however. Even Millie, who at the time, was only 6.

After drying my eyes a touch, I scooted down to grab some food. Everywhere I looked I could see very obvious 'MDSers.' As I would find, MDSers come in many different shapes and sizes, however what made everyone stand out, was that each and every one of us was wearing our most precious of possessions: our running shoes. These were the one item none of us could afford to lose, so the safest option was to wear them. Looking around, there were dozens and dozens of running shoes with the tell-tale Velcro strips. I wasn't feeling particularly sociable though, so didn't strike up any conversations and nestled myself into a corner of a Giraffe restaurant, and read the paper. The truth is, I wasn't feeling anti-social. I was feeling over-awed and intimidated. All of a sudden I was that 14 year old boy again, sitting in the pen before the English Schools 800m, looking at all of the other boys thinking 'he looks quicker than me. He *definitely* looks fitter than me.' I started doubting my credibility for being there. They all seemed so confident, and seemed to know each other. There was lots of backslapping, and greeting of long lost friends. *What the fuck had I been thinking?* How could I have been so arrogant as to think I could rub shoulders with these people? Maybe I could miss the plane, and save face?!

This level of self-doubt was nothing new, and I knew how to deal with it. I'd experienced the same thing before just about every running event I'd done, ever since I was a small boy. It would possibly surprise those who know me, and know me to be an outgoing, confident person, but life's full of contradictions. Even when I was a junior and winning most races I was entering, I'd still fret beforehand about how it was likely to go. I remember reading how the former heavyweight boxing champion, Floyd Patterson used to go to fights armed with a disguise so that, should he lose, he could vacate the venue without anyone noticing. I could understand this. It took me years to be able calmly rationalise my thinking, and be able to 'talk myself down.' I'd tell myself that I'd done well in my previous races, and therefore I was reasonably likely to do well in whatever race I was panicking about. Here, scanning the terminal, I tried telling myself the same thing. 'You did well at Pilgrims, you're going to be fine.' But in this pressure cooker environment, it didn't do much good. I was worried that I was never going to sleep at the hotel, and this was going to be my last night in a bed for a while! I decided to order a glass of wine, with a view to nodding off more quickly. I drank this whilst reading the paper and remaining amazed at the sheer volume of MDSers milling around; it was like we were taking over the airport. I returned to my hotel, set three separate alarms (I didn't *really* want to miss the flight!) and got my head down.

CHAPTER 11

I actually slept pretty well, and enjoyed what would be my last shower for a while. I got dressed, text my wife and sauntered down into the terminal. Even at 5am, it was pretty busy, and as I turned a corner to the check in desk for our chartered Titan Airways flight to Ouarzazate, I was taken aback by the long line of MDSers queueing to check into our flight. There were literally hundreds of runners queued up, all chatting nervously. I spotted various faces that I had seen at previous Ultras and nodded and smiled at each one. I felt extremely uneasy though; as if I needed a longer notice period to prepare myself to be ready to speak with them. What sort of notice was I thinking of exactly? I'd signed up 2 years ago, and been planning on entering for the previous 20 years! As I neared the front of the line, I spotted Paul, who was one of my tent mates. He looked to be in a similar frame of mind to me. We exchanged 'Hellos' and checked in. We walked through to departures and met up with the rest of our tent, or at least, another 4 of the 8 who would make up Tent 143. This was a big moment. Anyone who has done the MDS will tell you; choose your tent mates wisely. Great tent mates will help you along the way. Bad tent mates can make the week a living hell. Whilst I had chatted to my tent buddies over whatsapp, I hadn't actually met any of them other than Paul. I was now about to find out whether they were going to help the week go smoothly, or about to make it a week of purgatory.

They were great! I warmed to all of them instantly, and as I shook hands with them all, made a note to myself that I wanted to be sure to come across like a 'positive person.' I wanted them to be reassured that I'd be 'cup half full' all week, and encouraging them along. Whether this came across or not, I don't know, but we all seemed to rub along quite well from the start. I've read MDS books where people have psycho-analysed each of their tent mates in turn. This seems improper in the extreme, to me. The MDS is an intensely personal and also intimate experience. Most people barely know their tent mates before arriving in the desert, yet within 24 hours are all sleeping in a row, rubbing shoulders. You see each other in various states of undress, discuss the most personal of toilet habits, and chafing in the most sensitive of areas. Far more than this though, you share your most personal of dreams, fears and motivations, and bare your soul to these people. When out in the desert, people you have hitherto never met, will sob on your shoulder and tell you personal details they probably wouldn't tell their closest friends. In many ways, the superficial and fleeting nature of your relationship, along with the intensity of the task in hand, allows this to happen. There goes a saying in rugby circles that 'what goes on tour stays on tour.' And that is how I shall approach the detail of characters in Tent 143. Whilst obviously, they play a vital role in my story, and will feature throughout, I don't wish to betray the sanctity and perfection of the relationship we enjoyed by sullying it with cheap analysis here. It's important to the narrative of the story, however, that I set out who was in the tent.

Paul – I'd met Paul running the Pilgrims, and it was he who had introduced me to the majority of the tent. With a cycling background, Paul had completed an Ironman so was clearly in fantastic physical and mental condition. A similar age to me, Paul was expecting twins back home which was a source of interest within the tent.

Mark – the youngest in the tent and clearly in outstanding nick. Mark had done the Isle of Wight challenge (66 miles) in one go which merited serious respect.

Jorge – whilst Spanish, Jorge joined our tent as he told the organisers he lived in England (which he does). A few years older than me, Jorge's a regular action man; loving running, surfing, kite surfing and life in general.

Dee – Dee was taking on the MDS as part of her 50th birthday celebrations. She was a running machine and had clearly trained exceptionally hard – including hot weather training. Dee's beaming personality made her a joy to be around and a real motivating force.

Julian – Jules was very experienced. Nothing seemed to phase him. He'd done a variety of long distance runs, including the Centurion Grand Slam – 4x 50 mile races in one year. Impressive stuff.

Charlotte – I liked Charlotte within seconds of meeting her. I doubt she would mind me describing her as quiet, and hope she wouldn't mind me describing her as very evidently as hard as nails. Charlotte and Jules were running buddies from back home and had done the majority of their training together.

Duncan – a similar age to me, and evidently in outstanding physical condition. Duncan was to become a bigger part of my MDS journey than I could ever have imagined.

We exchanged a few tales and gently sensed each other out. Who was the most experienced? Who was likely to fare well? It was all good humoured, and good fun. An early decision was that we couldn't cope with having two 'Duncans' in the tent. I therefore offered to go by 'Nellie' which is an old school nickname, that I'm still known by to a few people, so I knew I'd respond to it!

As we boarded the plane, we all split up and sat in our pre-arranged seats. I sat down next to a chap who was in his mid-fifties. He'd taken a loan out to fund his ticket. He explained that it was a one time only attempt for him. I was instantly humbled. I'd told myself it was a one time only attempt for me as well, but I'm not sure I really meant it. In fact, I know I *didn't* mean it. At 40 years old, I had time on my side, and realistically, if needs be, I could scrape the money together for another attempt. But here was a guy who was very, very clear in his assertion that it was 'shit or bust.' As we sat there chatting about our dreams of collecting a winner's medal, and how disconsolate we would be if we didn't make it to the finish line, it got me thinking.... Who on the plane was destined not to make it all the way? I found myself scanning the heads in front of me... 'He looks fit, he'll finish, she'll *definitely* finish.' It suddenly dawned on me that I was basically a virtual grim reaper. I wondered how many people had looked at my head and considered whether I'd finish or not. And more importantly, what decision they had come to!

The matter of 'finishing or not' throws up a key dynamic. Any MDSer will explain the dilemma of Competing vs Completing. i.e. Do you take a more risky approach, and push things hard, in an attempt to get yourself higher up the field, but potentially blow up and not finish. Or do you approach things more cautiously to guarantee a finish, but potentially not ultimately finish as high up the field as you could. It was a tricky balance. I'd publicly stated that I was just there to collect a finisher's medal and that anything else would be a bonus. Secretly, I hoped for a top 50% finish, but I was 100% committed to not risking finishing by going out too hard in the pursuit of this. As my tent mates and I kept saying to each other as we discussed this dilemma in detail. 'If someone tells you they've done the MDS, you never ask them what position they finish in – you just bow down in reverence.' So whilst I would ideally love to finish in the top half, I was 100% committed to finishing. I would rather finish in last place than collapse 10 metres from the finish line, placed higher up the field. This appeared to be the approach of many. From my point of view, I was so incredibly paranoid about the effects of the heat that I just could not predict how my body was going to react when out on the course. I may fly along, but equally, I may struggle from first step to last.

When we arrived in Ouazazarte, we disembarked the plane and proceeded to wait at passport control. This was the first experience of one of the key features of the MDS – hanging around. You really do spend an awful lot of time waiting. The good news is, you don't really have anything else to do, so it's not as irritating as it would be in your everyday life. And in many respects this is one of the most joyous elements of the MDS. Once you step foot on the plane to Morocco, all you are there to do is run. Your whole trip is geared around running, and nothing else really matters. In an everyday world where 3G, 4G, wifi, mobiles, emails, facebook, twitter... (the list goes on) dominate, the pure basic pleasure of existence when all that matters is getting from A to B is both exhilarating and liberating. Normally, I'd be pissed off if I was kept waiting, but here it didn't matter. There was no point checking my phone for messages, as I had no signal. Similarly, email was out. And, dare I say it, as a dad of a 6 and 4 year old, it was quite refreshing to not have the constant *'dad, dad, dad, dad'* commentary in my ear! So it all became about enjoying the moment, enjoying what would be incredible scenery, and enjoying the company of this diverse group of people around me.

The queue to get through baggage reclaim and security was considerable. It took us another hour before we eventually started filing out through the exit, and it was here that we first met Patrick Bauer, who is Mr MDS. He is the race director, and remains extremely hands on. He shook hands and kissed every single person who filed through the door. As I shook hands with him, I noticed a TV camera filming the proceedings. I'd love to say that I barely gave it any thought, such was my supercool demeanour, but it made me grin and gave me a bounce in my step. It made me feel I was part of something significant.

We stood outside waiting to be told which coach to board. As we stood there I considered the temperature. 'This isn't *too* bad!' I thought to myself. No sooner had I thought this, however, and someone muttered 'apparently it's a shit load hotter out in the desert.' Pop went that bubble of hope. We boarded the coach, and true to form, sat on the tarmac without moving, for 90 minutes. We then set off in the direction of the Sahara. This took an absolute age, and also involved us stopping to eat the provided packed lunch at the side of the road. As the coach stopped, we all walked 50 metres or so off the road, and sat ourselves down on the ground. The ground was hard and scattered with stones around the size of a cricket ball. I remember looking at them and thinking 'I hope we don't have to run through anything like this.' Little did I know!

After eating our meal, we returned to the coach. I thought we'd be at the camp soon enough, but just before the light started to fade, the coach stopped with little explanation. After half an hour or so, we realised that they were scheduling the coaches into the camp. By this point it was now pitch black. It was a little annoying, but as I've explained, 'waiting' is a key component of the MDS, so we just sat back and enjoyed the down time.

There was a lot of rumours flying around, before departure, about how you ensure you get yourself in a tent with your desired tent buddies. In actual fact, it is very simple. The organisers came on the coach, asked if we were in groups, and organised accordingly. By this point, we had gained a seventh member, and they told us to send one person to take care of the admin, at camp check in, whilst the others dealt with the bags. And that was that. It really was that simple. In my experience, this was just the first example of areas that were not to be anywhere near as tricky as I had feared. It was the first, yet not the last, example of how, with the MDS the prospect is typically more daunting than the reality. I went ahead and checked us in, and we dragged our bags through to Tent 143.

For the uninitiated amongst you, the MDS bivouac is something to behold. The tents that competitors sleep / live in are set out in 3 decreasing circles, one within the other. The precision with which it appears to be set out is remarkable. The official camera crew provide aerial photographs of the bivouac and it is quite amazing to observe. And now, following months if not years of preparation, here we were. Or, more selfishly, here I was.

For the first two nights, the organisers lay on food for you. There are dining tents set up, and large buffet style meals. The food is traditional Moroccan cuisine and very nice indeed. Some people choose not to eat the food due to fears over picking up germs, or the food not agreeing with them. In contrast, all of the members of Tent 143 gleefully tucked in to our dinner whilst chatting nervously. I was starting to become extremely nervous. Everywhere I looked there appeared to be people better prepared than me. My tent mates were fantastic however; all very friendly and very humble. There was no preening, and I'm sure they were just as nervous as me. We finished our food and returned to our tent with a view to having an early night.

I should probably take some time to explain the detail of the tents. Whilst in the desert, your accommodation is a side-less Berber tent. It has a thick hessian mat that is laid straight onto the ground, and it is up to each competitor whether they sleep directly on top of the mat, or uses some kind of sleeping mat. The team who erect all of the tents do their best to remove any large rocks, however small stones remain, and the unwritten rule in the desert is that those first back to the tent each day roll back the mat and sweep out any offending rocks, before replacing the mat. Having no sides, the tent offers up limited protection from the wind, and also the cold!

I had taken with me a traditional swimming pool lilo. I used this for the first two nights, before binning it on the morning of the first race day. It meant that I had a bit more comfort on these two nights – something that was to be in short supply during the race itself. I inflated my lilo and climbed into my Yeti sleeping bag. Before long, I dropped off to sleep but awoke at 1am as I was uncomfortably cold. I had taken a sleeping bag liner with me, but was hoping to put it in my bag that they return to hotel awaiting our return, to keep my pack weight down. I realised however that I would have to take it with me. Even with the liner I was still cold, so I ended up sleeping in leggings, my long-sleeved race top, a down jacket, and a liner. Even then I wasn't particularly warm, but was able to sleep.

The next morning, I woke at 5:30am. This tends to be the time most people rise when in the bivouac. On waking up, I realised that I felt terrible. Simply put, I felt like I had a hangover. My head was pounding. I grabbed a bottle and drank half a litre of water straight down. I lay back down again confident that the headache would soon disappear. This was registration day so I didn't have to do anything particularly energetic, but I could do without a banging head. Unfortunately, however, my headache got worse, not better. I had an array of painkillers with me, but I didn't want to 'waste' them ahead of the race. Instead, I just tried to drink as much water as I could.

With each passing hour, and my headache not improving, I began to worry; there was no way I could run properly if I felt like this. I tried to forget about it and got on with the admin of the day. The registration process consists of a series of checks – of your identity, your ECG, and your pack weight. It also consists of a hell of a lot of waiting around – in the baking hot sun.

After handing over my 'return' bag to the crew, a lot of sitting down, a bit of pacing around and a nervous trot across the sand to see how my head felt (terrible), it was soon time for me to stand in the queue and wait my turn for my identity, ECG and pack to be checked. The order you are requested to attend the checks is determined by your race number. Unfortunately, by the time it was my 'turn,' it was the heat of the day, and the queue was both long and slow moving. I ended up stood in line waiting for approximately 90 minutes. I became increasingly pissed off. My head was thumping and I really wanted to be out of the sun. I reminded myself though that everyone was in the same boat, that there were no doubt others feeling far worse than me, and that generally speaking, I needed to stop being such a baby and embrace the whole experience.

When I eventually did make it to front of the line, I presented the doctor with my passport and ECG, whilst completing the questionnaire that was me confirming I had all of the mandatory items in my pack – and no doubt also signing my life away, should anything go wrong! The doctor inspected my pack for what seemed like an eternity. I'd say that I began to sweat, but I was already sweating buckets! After about 5 minutes though, she confirmed that I was good to go, they weighed my pack, and I moved through to the next desk where they gave me my number, water card and salt tablets, poo-bags and attached my tracking beacon to my pack.

There had been some light-hearted competition within our tent as to who had the lightest, and also the heaviest pack. My pack came in a fraction under 8kg, which was a real boost to my confidence given I wasn't feeling great. Being fair, I was wearing a kind of bum-bag where the pouch sits at the front, and had stashed a lot of gels in there, so my total pack-weight was in reality a little bit heavier than 8kg. Still, I was happy, and looked forward to the jokes when I got back to the tent.

The tracker that is attached to your pack is a mandatory item, and vital all ways round. This is a GPS device that alerts the crew if you venture off the official route when out on the course. If they spot you do this, they will monitor your progress, and send a rescue team if needs be. (In 1994, a chap called Mauro Prosperi got lost in the desert for 10 days after taking a wrong turn on the course. He only survived after drinking rats' blood and his own urine. I didn't particularly fancy drinking my own piss, so the GPS tracker was a welcome addition in this respect!) The further benefit is that it allows your loved ones back home to track your progress in real time.

When I got back to the tent there was the predicted jokes about each other's pack weights and nervous chatter. My head was still painful, and I eventually took the decision to pop a couple of paracetamol whilst also making my first trip to the MDS toilets.

'Toilet,' it turns out, is a fairly broad term. I'd read up on the MDS extensively before the trip, so had a good idea of what to expect. That said, the reality of the situation was slightly disappointing to say the least. The toilet block is a 'three trap' type affair, with each cubicle separated by fairly thin canvas. The toilet itself is like a plastic garden chair with a large hole in the middle of it. The idea is that you stretch your poo-bag over the seat, sit on it, and let nature do the rest. It's not quite as simple as that though, and early on, there were all sorts of horror stories being discussed around the bivouac. (One guy in the tent next to us filled a bag, only for a particularly strong gust of wind to empty the entire bag of piss and shit all over the only pair of trainers he had to wear for the entire week. Being honest, whilst shocking for him, we couldn't stop laughing for about an hour when we learned of his misfortune!)

The other big fear is illness. A cursory glance around the inside of the cubicle I found myself in showed all sorts of upsetting looking stains on the walls, as well as what was quite clearly human waste on the ground. I decided that wherever possible, I would not bother with the toilet block and disappear off over a sand-dune, to avoid any germs. On this, first occasion, however, I negotiated the toilet without too much issue, drenched myself in anti-bac hand gel and returned to camp. There was much japery whenever someone returned from the toilet. 'How was it?!' would come the question. There was mild disappointment when I announced that I hadn't encountered any catastrophes.

That night, we went to the food tent for our last meal that would be laid on for us. When I was there, I took the opportunity to swipe a few paper napkins, just in case I didn't have enough toilet paper during the week! As I did so, I felt a little embarrassed; as if this act was an admission that I may not be as well prepared as I should be. I pushed the thought to the back of my mind.

We sat down as a tent-group and broke bread together. It was a heart-warming moment. We were all from different backgrounds, were very different people, but all had this impending adventure in common. We had all sacrificed a lot; had worried a lot, and had shared a similar dream. Who knew how the week would pan out for each of us. I looked at my tent mates, who I had already become very fond of. I remember staring wistfully into the stars, and being close to overcome by how very much I hoped we would all be successful against whatever goals and expectations we had set ourselves.

Before long, it was time to return to our tent and get our heads down ahead of, as I saw it, the biggest challenge of my life. My head was still very painful as I arranged my pack ready for the morning. I put my breakfast near the top, and my essential items such as number, strapping and water underneath my pack. I climbed into my sleeping back, said goodnight to my tent mates, and closed my eyes. Being a staunch atheist, it would be a lie to say I 'prayed,' but I certainly lay there, hoping with all my might, that my headache would dissipate. Before long, I dropped off to sleep.

CHAPTER 12

All men dream: but not equally. Those who dream by night in the dusty recesses of their minds wake in the day to find that it was vanity: but the dreamers of the day are dangerous men, for they may act their dreams with open eyes, to make it possible.
T. E. Lawrence

Day 1 – 30.3 KM

I woke up nervous. My first thought was 'how's my head?' The answer was, pretty good. In fact, no headache at all. I lifted it up and gave it a fairly vigorous shake. Nothing; no pain at all. Get in!! This race was happening! I got up, brushed my teeth, cooked my breakfast, which consisted of granola, and began taping my feet and shoulders. I also drank as much as I could, taking care to check my wee was clear.

That first morning was incredible. The atmosphere was electric; you could feel the nerves within the camp. The vast majority of us had no idea what we were about to encounter, and you could sense the trepidation. Looking around the camp, I felt there were a few people there who would gladly have accepted if you'd offered them a guilt-free exit at that point. I had been in the exact same place, mentally, the day before. Today though, I was bouncing. I couldn't wait! This was what it had all been about. I was in my element. I thought of Lucy and the kids; of them at home going about their everyday lives, and me here in a totally alien environment, about to embark upon the adventure of a lifetime. I knew Lucy would be thinking of me, and I smiled to myself. Eventually, we headed over towards the start line as dictated by the organisers. We were shepherded to stand together, in order to make up the number 33, to denote this as being the 33rd edition of the race. Once we had assembled, a helicopter hovered above, allowing them to take a photo for publicity purposes.

We then headed towards the start line itself. Patrick Bauer, the Race Director, began his daily briefing, and well wishing. Some people became frustrated with how long this would take each morning, but I loved it. I'd read all about this in advance, and here I was, in a dusty desert, with a thousand other runners, about to start the race of my life. Soon enough, the music started. Initially, 'Let's Stay Together' by Al Green blasted out of the PA system, and then 'Highway to Hell,' by ACDC. I stood there, bouncing up and down on my toes. I felt a million dollars. I cannot describe the feeling of belonging and excitement I experienced at that moment. After all of the work and the worry, I was actually on the start line to the MDS! And then at just after 8am, Patrick counted down 'DIX, NEUF, HUIT, SEPT, SIX, CINQ, QUATRE, TROIS, DEUX, UN, GOOOOOOOOO!' We were off!

I had intentionally positioned myself towards the rear end of the field on the start. I figured this would reduce the chances of me falling victim to my typical inability to pace myself properly. I thought that having lots of runners in front of me would force me to run at a more measured pace. I started to trot as the runners ahead of me moved forwards, and within thirty seconds or so, I had crossed the start line and was underway. I was doing it! I was actually DOING IT!! No matter what happened now, I had got myself to the start line in one piece. I was running in the Marathon Des Sables! My headache was gone, I felt great, and I was underway. The first thing I noticed was that the heat wasn't actually that bad. Sure, it was hot; very hot. But it wasn't actually that oppressive. The dry nature of the heat seems to make it more bearable, and one of my biggest fears, if not my *biggest* fear was playing out ok. Granted, it was still very early in the morning, but it wasn't quite panic stations yet.

I ran along fairly gingerly to start with, telling myself not to worry about the huge group of runners in front of me. Rather pick up places as the day went on, than have others pick you off, I had told myself. Very quickly, however, I noticed a problem with my pack. It was putting pressure on my right clavicle in a way that it had never done before. It wasn't too bad though, so I carried on. Suddenly, out of nowhere, all thoughts of my shoulder were forgotten when I felt a sharp pain in my right foot. It was like I had stood on a drawing pin. I stopped instantly, mindful of all of the guidance to address any issues encountered, instantly. I looked at my watch; I had been running for less than 1km. I took my shoe off to find that a thorn had gone straight through the sole of my trainer and into my foot. Whilst I was dealing with my shoe, Mark from my tent ran past, pausing to check if I was ok. I replied that I was and sent him on his way. I managed to pull the thorn out of the sole of my shoe before putting my shoe back on and returning to a run. As I was running, I began to panic; after all my internal wrangling over my footwear, I'd clearly chosen the wrong pair. I couldn't believe I'd made such a stupid mistake. Less than 1km into a 250km race and my shoes had let me down. Or more to the point, I had let myself down. I found myself trying to place my feet very carefully to avoid a repeat performance.

Now my pack began to hurt my shoulder. A lot. I didn't panic though, and put my hand underneath that strap, telling myself I'd deal with it when I got to the first check point. I was fare more worried about how my shoes were going to hold up.

Within ten minutes, another issue became apparent. Rumblings in my stomach, and an all too familiar feeling 'down below' suggested all was not well. Most long-distance runners will talk of the dreaded 'need a poo' runs. Sometimes, the rhythmic motion of running can encourage your body to need the toilet. I deduced that this, along with the local cuisine for the last two nights, had given me something of an issue. Whatever the cause though, I'd gone from feeling fantastic, to being in a situation with a thorn in my foot, a backpack that was beyond painful, and an arse that wanted to explode. And I hadn't even run 5km yet. I was feeling rather despondent. Only half an hour after feeling on top of the world at the start line, now it felt like everything might be over before it had even begun. I trudged on, reminding myself that the checkpoint was my opportunity to address my situation.

The terrain was predominantly compacted sand, before turning into fairly small dunes. There were quite a few inclines that needed climbing and also some areas of rocks that needed to be carefully negotiated. There were a lot of runners ahead of me. I calculated that having started towards the back, stopped to remove my shoe, and then run/walk at a very steady pace to stop my pack from hurting, I would be very far down the field. After 1 hour and 42 minutes I reached the first check point. By this point, I was in desperate need of the toilet. As I entered the check point, I asked an official, who told me to 'make pee-pee over there.' I laughed and said that it was a bit more serious than that. She laughed back, shrugged, and pointed out over the dunes. I didn't need telling twice, and climbed up over the nearest sand dune, in search of some privacy.

I appreciate the following isn't particularly pleasant, but I promised I'd offer up a 'warts and all' account of my experience. My main concern was to not end up coated in my own shit, so I tried to work the angles in my favour. The ensuing bowel movement was spectacular in its ferocity, but thankfully I remained unscathed. Just at this moment, the press helicopter flew over the top of me. I began to laugh... this was ridiculous! I'd dreamed of running this race for half my life, and now I was here, I was in danger of being caught on camera, decimating the desert! It took me a while to put myself back together, whilst also kicking sand over the offending area.

I walked back to the check point, sat down and removed my shirt. I fumbled around in my pack for an eternity before locating some heavy strapping that I had packed, along with one of those thin sponges they sell in the UK, for use when cleaning. I strapped the sponge to my shoulder and then put my kit back on. This took a fair while, and I had to enlist the help of a charitable fellow runner who put the strapping in the right place.

The padding of the sponge seemed to do the trick. I re-joined the race and began jogging. The only issue was that my bout of diarrhoea had wiped me out, and I felt pretty weak. I cursed how much time I had lost whilst at the checkpoint. Looking at my watch, I had lost nearly an hour. This irritated me a great deal. It was at this point that I made what was to be a key pact with myself. For the rest of the week, no matter what I had to do whilst out on the course, I would do it whilst moving forwards. I *had* to keep moving forwards. This represented a major moment for me mentally. Whilst only a subtle change in thinking, it meant that I knew that whatever I was doing, I was getting closer to the finish line, and therefore to my goal. The steps, no matter how small, were heading in the right direction.

The course soon morphed into bigger sand dunes. After approximately 20km, I began to feel a bit better, and it was at this point that I found myself walking through deep sand with Rory Coleman. I reminded Rory who I was (from his brother doing my ECG) and had a long chat with him. Being from the same part of Warwickshire, originally, we had some shared friends. It was nice to talk with him, and I felt some reassurance from being in his presence. Whilst Rory isn't (now) known for his pace out on the course at the MDS, that I was still keeping up with him, despite my fairly disastrous start, gave me some comfort.

After a couple of kilometres, I bade farewell to Rory, and tried to pick the pace up a bit. I next encountered a corporate lawyer from Hong Kong, who had put his career on hold in order to focus on the MDS. He was an extremely bright, articulate guy, and it was enjoyable spending some time in his company, whilst ticking off a few more kilometres. It was whilst I was with Mr Lawyer, that I encountered my first awe-inspiring view of the Sahara. We ran to the top of a dune, that turned into a hard ridge. I could see a line of runners ahead of me, and individually they all stopped to take in a view. When I reached the vantage point myself, the view was breath-taking. In many ways, the Sahara is more like a moonscape than a landscape. It is so baron that it appears to be from another world. This, coupled with the fact that you can see for miles, is quite awe-inspiring. I was brought down to earth, however, when I saw a long line of runners, stretching quite literally, miles in front of me. They looked like a colony of ants, and it made me realise both how far I still had to go, and where I stood in the field.

I entered Checkpoint 2 at 3hrs39m. I took my water, allowed the official to stamp my water-card and began refilling my water bottles. As I did so, I kept walking along the course, slowly towards the large bin. (In the MDS they write your bib number on your bottles of water and anyone who is found to have discarded their empty bottles anywhere other than in an official bin, receives a time penalty.) I dropped an isotonic tablet into my left hand bottle, and left the right bottle as pure water. This was my tactic throughout the race. Tossing my empty bottle into the bin, I began to jog and picked off a few runners who were ahead of me.

The truth is, I was feeling rather lonely at this point. The camaraderie of my chats with Rory and Mr Lawyer were long forgotten, and I felt pretty vulnerable. The day hadn't gone particularly well thus far, and I was feeling a bit of a fraud. I'd trained really hard, sacrificed a lot, yet was now struggling due to a thorn in my foot, a painful backpack, and a bad dose of Delhi Belly. This wasn't a great situation; not by a long way! Being honest, I was just feeling a bit vulnerable and in need of something to get myself back on track mentally. I doubled down on my efforts and pushed towards the finish line. The terrain went from dunes back to more compact sand, and I began to pick up the pace a touch. I started to focus on the positives; yes, I'd had a few issues, but thorn aside, my feet hadn't given me any issues at all. I had no 'hot-spots' on my feet, and based on the colour of my wee, was fully hydrated. Despite the fact that it was now around midday, the heat was still manageable, and most importantly, I was moving forward. I kept telling myself this wasn't a sprint; nor was it a marathon... it was a multi-day ultra-marathon!

As the topography of the terrain flattened out, I caught a glimpse of the inflatable finishing gantry in the distance. I couldn't gauge how far away it was, but seeing it gave me a boost. I estimated that it was about a mile away, but in reality, it turned out to be triple that. This was the first time I was to experience how the barren landscape of the desert seriously impacts on your sense of perspective. I quickly learned that it was wise to not try to gauge a distance based on your eyes. I wasn't alone, it became a regular topic of discussion in the bivouac, and most people seemed to struggle with this. It wasn't a big deal however, as ultimately we all knew the length of each stage, and most people were wearing GPS watches so it was fairly simple maths to work things out.

I focused on catching up with a few more competitors before the finish line. The motivation for this was two-fold. The main reason being, it gave me something to focus on, and smaller, more immediate goals than the finish line that never appeared to move any closer. The associated bi-product was that it improved my position in the field. I eventually crossed the finish line after 5hrs1m. I had actually picked my pace up considerably towards the end of the stage, and ended up running between two runners right on the line. I felt a bit foolish for doing so afterwards. The seconds I had gained in doing so really were inconsequential, and I felt bad for interrupting their moment of crossing the line.

As I crossed the line, I noticed there was a webcam pointing at the finish. I self-consciously ran straight past it without any acknowledgment, and gratefully took a cup of the sweet local tea they provide all runners with. I am sure that it would be sickly sweet on a normal day in England, but after a long run in the desert, it is perfect to give you a quick sugar injection. I took my 6 litres of water which was to last me until the first checkpoint the next day, and walked into the bivouac.

The first thing that struck me was how busy it was, and how many people were already back. I knew I hadn't had a great day but seeing so many people already back with their feet up was a sobering sight. As I've said previously, my actual position didn't matter to me a great deal, but I was worried that maybe I wasn't up to the task. If I was low down the field on the first day, would that mean that I may struggle to make it through the week? Would I be one of the ones who wouldn't make it? My sense of worry and vulnerability wasn't helped by how cheerful everyone else seemed. I find it embarrassing to admit, but as I walked, I felt a deep sense of shame. I felt as if all eyes were on me, wondering what had gone wrong. *The reality was, of course, that no-one was remotely interested in me but try telling me that at the time!*

Eventually, I found Tent 143. It felt so good to be back with my tent mates. I was fifth back, and was so grateful to be in their company. The benefit of not being first back meant that my comrades had already swept under the mat for any stones, so I was able to throw my pack down and lie down with my feet rested on my backpack. It was such a relief to be off my feet. We discussed how each other's day had gone. There was genuine concern about my thorn-in-the-foot situation, and much amusement about my toilet incident at checkpoint 1. My tent mates all seemed very happy with how their day had gone. My sense of unease grew. It wasn't that I was unhappy with how the day had gone – I mean, I *was* unhappy with how it had gone, but also, I was becoming increasingly fearful of how the rest of the week was going to go.

I busied myself with getting some recovery food inside of me, in a bid to both take my mind of things, and commence the basic recovery process. A while later, our tent was complete with the arrival of Jorge, and then Jules and Charlotte. Jules and Charlotte were evidently good friends from back in England, and had completed many ultra-challenges together. They had set their stall out early during our expedition; they were planning on walking the entire thing. They were an extraordinary pair. Despite the fact that they were evidently amongst the slower people out on the course, they were clearly as hard as nails. If you had asked me at the start of the race who within our tent I would put my life on to finish the course, it would have been these two. They came back in, and instantly injected a bit of life into the tent. Jules in particular was good for a laugh and a joke, and I began to cheer up.

After an hour or so, I opened up to the tent and told them how disappointed I was with how my day had gone. They sympathised, and I suddenly felt ashamed for feeling so down. I told myself to pull myself together, and went for a wander around the bivouac to give my legs a stretch. As I did, Duncan, one of my tent mates caught me up. He had been first back to our tent that day, so it was useful to talk with him about how his day had gone. After a while, he said 'do you fancy running together tomorrow?' He was very honest; he felt that he'd gone off too quickly on Day 1, and could understand that I'd probably not done myself justice. He felt that in reality, he should be running slower, and I should be running quicker, so joining forces made logical sense. I felt overwhelmed by the generosity of his offer. I must have asked him 7 times if he was sure, and each time he calmly said 'yes mate, of course.'

I've previously said that I won't psycho-analyse any of my tent friends, but Duncan became such an integral part of my journey that it's impossible to properly describe later events without talking you through him, and me, and the relationship that was formed. Duncan's an extremely bright, engaging guy. Softly spoken, and level headed, he has an inner-steel that captured my imagination. In many ways, he and I were to develop a type of Ying and Yang type relationship. I am more outgoing; he is more reserved. He probably has more self-restrain than I do. I had instantly warmed to the guy, and when he offered me the opportunity to run with him, I felt an instant boost to my morale.

When Duncan and I returned to the tent I set about cooking my evening meal. I gathered a collection of fuel tablets in my stove and set fire to them. I then poured some water into my pot and placed the lid on. The expression states that a 'watched pot never boils,' but in fact, my pot came to a boil relatively quickly. I'd cut an empty water bottle in half and put my free-dried chilli and rice into the bottom half. I poured the water in, gave it a stir and left the water to rehydrate the food. (This tactic ensures you don't have to wash up your pot, and can just throw away dirty half-bottle.) Fifteen minutes or so later, I was greedily tucking into my dinner. It tasted fantastic! I ate every last morsel and washed it down with a litre of water, and a Grenade Bar. Before leaving, I had parceled up a small amount of Peanut M&Ms and Haribo for each day. I thought it would be motivating to have something to look forward to whilst out on the course. That first night though, I put my bag of treats back into my pack unopened. I didn't feel that I had earned them that day, and told myself I'd enjoy them the following day.

Early in the evening, they pinned the day's results up on the noticeboard on the entrance to the camp. I had finished in 608th place. This was about what I had guestimated when I walked through the camp. Seeing it in black and white disappointed me all the same. I told myself not to dwell on it, and vowed to do better the next day. I then queued up for use of the laptops set up to allow you to email home. I sent an email to Lucy telling her how I had completed the first day successfully, but was a bit disappointed, and planned to do better. I probably sugar coated my emotions a bit. For some reason, I didn't want her to be disappointed in my disappointment.

That evening we all lay in the tent and chatted about general nonsense. It turned out Jules and I had a shared love of 80s/90s dance and hip hop music and we talked through our favourite artists. It was wonderfully liberating to be simply lying down talking, without any of the interruptions that are so accepted in our every day lives back home. Soon enough, it was time to get our heads down and we all climbed into our sleeping bags. Just as we did so, however, the post lady arrived! A fantastic characteristic of the MDS is the ability of supporters back home to send you messages when you are out on the course. The organisers print them off and deliver them to your tents. It was just what I needed; a few messages from friends, and a note from my mum, one from Lucy, one from my 6 year old daughter Millie, and one from my 4 year old son, Ted (dictated to Lucy!).

It was Millie's note that had the greatest effect on me. She had the perfect combination of understanding of what I was trying to do, and naivety of how hard it actually was. For a 6 year old, Millie is pretty articulate and she wrote simply and in a matter of fact fashion, about what had happened to her in her day, and what her hopes were for me. Millie used a turn of phrase in this first email that would crop up in every mail she sent me. 'Good luck for tomorrow daddy. I just know you can do it.' Her wide-eyed belief and confidence in me hardened my resolve. Of course, her confidence was based on nothing other than the fact I am her daddy and in her eyes, therefore, I am invincible. But the sheer innocence of it took me aback.

After reading my messages, I fell asleep fairly quickly, however woke due to two reasons. The first being that I desperately needed a wee, and secondly because my sleeping mat had deflated, and I was extremely uncomfortable. I did my best to extricate myself from the tent without waking up my buddies, pushed my feet into my trainers and strolled away from the camp. I went for a wee and returned. It was 1am. I realised that I couldn't easily inflate my sleeping mat without waking everyone up, so resigned myself to a fairly uncomfortable night's sleep. And that is exactly what I endured, however I think this would be the case whether the mat had been fully inflated or not. It became an exercise in rotating, throughout the night, from one pressure point to another. I'd lie on my side for a while, and then wake up because it was uncomfortable, so rotate to my back, and then my other side, and then my front... It wasn't a

problem however, and in many ways I enjoyed the harsh experience –
it made me really feel like I was experiencing the true desert.

CHAPTER 13

Day 2 - 39km

I woke up at 4:45am, incredibly stiff. I pulled the hood of my sleeping bag over my head and tried to sneak a few more minutes rest before the start of the day. My tent mates started to stir. Jules was lying next to me and sat up. 'Hello mate,' he whispered. I gave him a smile. 'Morning buddy.' I joined him by sitting up. Good grief my back was stiff! The sun had just started to rise, and the view of the silhouettes of all of the tents was striking. The chatter in the bivouac got louder, and soon enough everyone was up and about. I set off on what was to become a morning ritual: walk out to the bush to go for a wee. Return to the tent to brush my teeth, and prepare my breakfast. All whilst drinking as much water as I possibly could.

Looking around the bivouac, it struck me how different people had such different approaches to preparation on the day. Some would carry out extremely impressive stretching routines. Some would go on warm up runs. Others would simply lie down until the last possible moment. My approach was to stroll around and carry out some light stretching.

I spoke to Duncan again and asked if he was still happy to run as a pair. He confirmed he was. We all then began packing up our packs and completing final preparations. I had taken to using Gurney Goo which is designed to prevent chafing. It worked remarkably well, however it did necessitate the application of the 'Goo' around all sorts of personal areas, when there was little shelter to protect one's modesty.

We gathered at the start line, and Patrick began his customary pre-race address. Patrick's a good guy; he's wonderfully enthusiastic, and generous with his spirit. He does, however, like the lengthy use of a microphone. Some people became quite agitated by his lengthy speeches. I quite liked them though. For me, it was all part of the experience. Every day, he would seem to find someone who was celebrating their birthday, and spin out his speech to include a birthday message to them! Soon enough though, Highway To Hell started up, and we were off.

It felt great to be running *with* someone. We set off at a sensible pace. The sort of pace when you can talk comfortably. Duncan and I shared stories about our lives. We have children of a similar age and enjoyed telling each other about them. It was instantly easy being with Duncan. Sometimes we'd talk; other times we'd be silent. There was no awkwardness; we both seemed to understand the rules of engagement. We were there to support each other. The terrain was relatively firm underfoot for the first section of the day. I realised that I was tending to move ahead of Duncan – typically building up a 10-15 metre gap between us, before I would realise and then drop back. Duncan was monitoring his heart rate, and was keen to keep it below 125bpm. If it ever went above this, he would ease off a touch. Whilst I had turned the heart rate monitor on my watch off, in order to preserve battery life, I liked this scientific approach. It made me feel that I was most definitely with the right man.

Looking back, I think that subconsciously, I was straining at the leash a touch on Day 2, as a direct result of my disappointing show the previous day. It was so important therefore, that Duncan was there to 'keep me honest.' We reached the first checkpoint in 1hr31m, and it all felt very different to the day before. One of the things I noticed was that the runners around me appeared to be of a different calibre to Day 1. It concerned me a little that I may have been pushing too hard, but it felt so good, that I carried on at the same pace. Talking with Duncan, he felt good too, so we pushed on together. At the checkpoint, they offered up 3 litres of water. I had decided that I would always take all of the water offered. I filled both of my bottles and drank about half a litre straight down. I poured the remainder over my head and threw the empty bottles in the bin.

We pushed on at a walk, initially. Duncan wanted to have a snack which gave us an excuse to have a walk. It sounds strange, but I would feel guilty if I walked, so having an 'excuse' helped me mentally. Before long though, we were back up to a trot. The next leg involved a very long, flat, monotonous section. This was relatively tough because the landscape was so baron, you could not use any landmarks to gauge progress. It felt like we weren't getting anywhere. In reality, I think this section lasted approximately 45 minutes, and we overtook a few people as we went.

It was at this point that I made a small but, fairly significant decision. I decided that any time I overtook someone, or someone overtook me, I would offer up words of encouragement. Everyone has their number and therefore their name, on their backpack, so it was very easy to jog past someone and call out 'good running Dave; looking good buddy!' Sometimes people would respond, even if it was just a thumbs up. Other times they wouldn't. From my point of view, whilst I was concerned with my overall performance, I didn't see myself as racing the other runners. I felt that we were all on a journey together, and all individually competing with ourselves, and specifically, the little voice in your head that was telling you to stop. A bit of encouragement here and there never did anyone any harm. It also meant they often returned the compliment, which was good for morale!

After the second checkpoint, the terrain turned to sand dunes. The dunes were very high, and very soft. They really sapped the energy from my legs. Each time you put your foot down, it sank back so, in reality, you were only taking half a pace, for every step made. I thought back to all of the work I had done in the gym and was grateful for all of the squat work I did with James. It was certainly being drawn on now. The truth of it is though, I absolutely loved the dunes. It was extremely hot, and I was knee deep in sand; this was what I had signed up for! Suddenly though we were thrown a bit of a curve ball. Out of the blue, Duncan's nose began pouring with blood! In actual fact, a lot of people suffered from nosebleeds. I assume it is because the breathing in of sand through the nose irritates the nose.

We stopped and I pulled out some of the napkins I had stashed in my pack the night before Day 1. It took about 5 minutes, but we managed to stop the flow of blood. We carried on, but very soon, the blood started again. We stopped again and I tried to offer some assistance. We stayed stationary for about 10 minutes, trying to stop the blood but it just kept coming. Eventually, Duncan laughed and told me to go on without him. I protested, but he was firm. He said he planned to walk for a while and that he didn't wish to slow me down. I felt torn; Duncan had shown me the generosity of spirit to offer to run with me when I was feeling down, and I wanted to repay him the support. He wouldn't entertain the idea however, and insisted I push on. I reluctantly bade him farewell, and as I ran off, said to myself that if I was going to leave him to run alone, I was going to make it worthwhile; I was going to push hard to the finish.

The course was about to get very interesting, as we approached a steep rocky climb. Whilst I felt bad for leaving Duncan, that I had done so injected me with renewed energy, drive and purpose. I felt unstoppable as I started up the climb. Ahead of my lay about 10 people, strung out. The terrain was challenging in terms of physical fitness, but not too technical. It was rather like climbing some very, very steep stairs. Underfoot was firm, so there were no issues there, and I relished the challenge of trying to 'pick off' the people ahead of me. This section of the course took approximately half an hour and I did, indeed, over take everyone I could see ahead of me, before reaching the peak and commencing the decline.

As I started to run downhill, I became aware of pain in the toes on my right foot. All of the advice is that if you feel any pain at all, you should stop, *instantly*, and deal with it. I figured I was nearly at the final checkpoint though, so decided to push on until then. I knew this was a bit of a risk but was willing to take it to maintain my momentum. I passed a few people as I went and pretty soon I was at Checkpoint 3. As I ran into the checkpoint I saw one man ahead of me. He looked the business in a yellow and red, Spanish themed tri-suit, and clearly exceptionally fit. I said 'hi' and asked him how he was going. He smiled back but said he was struggling a touch. I exited the checkpoint before him but started off walking whilst taking an energy gel. He ran up behind me, slapped me on my bum and said, 'no, we RUN!' I laughed and joined him in a run. It felt so incredibly motivating to be running with this guy I had never met before, who was quite clearly a decent runner, and who also seemed to be taking huge joy in the whole experience. After about a mile however, he said to me that he needed to walk for a bit, but that he wanted me to keep running.

I gave my Spanish friend a thumbs up and shouted 'good luck' before getting my head down. There was only around 4 miles to the finish and I was keen to get back and relax as soon as possible. By this point the toes on my right foot were seriously 'hot.' It felt like my nails were in trouble a touch. Looking back, I'm a little ashamed that I didn't stop to address the situation. The truth is however, that after my disappointing first day, my mental need to keep going outweighed my physical need to stop. I pushed on. The temperature was hot, but the terrain was fairly easy going. It was pretty flat, just with rocks scattered across the ground like a mini boulder field. At one point I kicked a reasonable sized rock with my painful foot. It felt like my toenails were being forced back into my toes. Still I kept going however.

Despite the pain in my foot, I was having the time of my life. There was nobody else within view ahead of me, and my Spanish comrade was now a long way behind. I thought back to Duncan; how was he? Had his nose stopped bleeding? Maybe he would catch me up and we could run in together? This didn't happen however, and I ran in on my own – although not before ultimately over-taking another two runners.

As I crossed the line, I felt good, and I felt like I had performed better. I had no idea how I had done, but I knew that I had fared better than the previous day, and importantly, had felt far stronger physically. After taking my water, and cup of sweet tea, I entered into the bivouac. The first thing I noticed was how few people were around. Looking into the tents, there were hardly any faces at all. The faces I did see belonged to very fit looking runners. After the disappointment of the previous day, I felt myself swelling with pride a touch. I'd held my own. When I arrived back at our tent, I found it empty. This both pleased and disappointed me. It pleased me as I had evidently done well out on the course, but disappointed me because it meant I had no-one to talk to! By this point, my feet were causing me quite serious grief. Before that though, I had an important task – the sweeping out of stones from under our tent mat. I took considerable pride in taking on the task, before taking my shoes off and inspecting my feet.

In actual fact, my toes weren't as bad as I had feared. I had blisters under two toenails, and the nails themselves had indeed been pushed backwards into my toes a touch. I slipped on my flip-flops, grabbed a recovery shake, and headed over to Doc Trotters – the on hand medical team. There was a short queue but soon enough I was inside the tent. The doctor asked me what the problem was and then directed me towards a bench where there was some disinfectant. He told me to wash my feet and then wait my turn.

I was actually seen within 10 minutes and explained to a second doctor what my problem was. I lay on my back on the floor and put my foot on her knees. She took out a sealed pack and then slid a scalpel blade underneath my toenails with the blisters. It was obviously extremely uncomfortable, but they had been uncomfortably anyway, so relatively speaking, it wasn't that bad. What was far worse, however, was when she dripped iodine into the blisters, and then pushed my toenails down to evacuate out the fluid. I did my best to laugh through it, but it was absolute agony. When she finished, she put strapping around the offending toes and sent me on my way. When I saw the strapping though, I was more than a little concerned. It was terrible! There was no way it would stand up to a full day's running the day after. On my way out of the tent, I asked if I could have some strapping to redo the strapping myself in the morning. The medical team granted this wish without any fuss, and I walked back to our tent.

On arriving at our tent, I found Duncan. We greeted each other warmly. He had taken it steady after we had separated, but was happy overall with how things had gone. I expressed my disappointment that we hadn't been able to complete the day together but we both knew that realistically, between us, we'd made the sensible decision. He had to slow down, but there was no point in me following suit unnecessarily. We sat and chatted about the bits on the course we'd liked, and the sections we'd found tough. Over the course of the next few hours, our tent gradually filled up. On this, the second day, there was now starting to be questions about potential drop outs. You could sense the mild tension as we waited for our outstanding tent mates, and the relief when each person walked up to the tent carrying their water, and invariably instantly lay down to take the weight off their legs. It was a mini-celebration when the tent became complete with the arrival of Charlotte & Jules.

We settled down into what was rapidly becoming my favourite part of the entire week; tired laughter at the day's developments. There was always something to smile or chuckle about, and I enjoyed hearing how other people had got on. It was amazing how a section I had found very tough, someone else had found very easy, and vice versa. We lay around the tent laughing. My mood was completely different to 24 hours before. Simply put, I felt that I had properly arrived at the MDS, and I now knew that I deserved to be there. My toes were throbbing, but I was happy.

After half an hour or so, I creaked to my feet and walked across to the email tent. There was still considerable heat within the sun, so I didn't wish to stay outside for too long, however when I exited our tent, I noticed people gathered around the noticeboard giving the results for the day. I took a detour and headed across, keen to see how I had done. I scanned down the results page and saw my name. I had come 206th on the day. I was absolutely over the moon. I'd hoped I had maybe come around the 350 mark, so to be this high was a major shock, and a fantastically positive one at that. I continued on my journey to the email tent with a faint bounce in my otherwise tired step. I wrote a heartfelt note to Lucy, explaining how much happier I was and how I was looking forward to the next day.

Back at the tent, I cooked my dinner of beef stroganoff and rice. Whilst it hadn't been as big an issue on day 2, my pack was still hurting my shoulder, so I was keen to shed weight in any way that I could. I therefore decided to jettison all of my cooking fuel. These are little tablets that look a bit like big energy tablets. They don't weigh a huge amount, but I was following the marginal gains school of thought, so out they went. My strategy was to instead use scrub and firewood that I would gather each night. It smoked a bit more, but in the grand schemes of things, this was totally inconsequential. As I sorted through my pack, I chatted to Dee who had endured a difficult day. She had fallen whilst negotiating a rocky area and damaged her hand. Having seen a variety of rugby injuries over the years, it looked highly likely to me that she had broken her finger. She was being remarkably relaxed about it though. She asked us what we thought, and whether we thought it was broken. I couldn't see much value in highlighting that I thought it probably was. What was she going to do with that information? I just said I thought she should strap it up and take pain killers. Her finger was massively swollen and she was evidently in a lot of pain, but she didn't moan at all. It was just another example of the mental fortitude of the people out on the course.

That night, as we all ate, conversation turned to our strategy for day 3. It turned out that everyone was in the same boat; the strategy for day 3 was designed with day 4 (the long day) in mind. We all agreed that it would be sensible to take things steady on day 3. I was absolutely shitting myself about day 4. I'd never run more than 36 miles in one go, so the full 52 was a big ask. It was essential, therefore, that I held a lot back during day 3, to ensure I went into day 4 with as full a tank as I could manage. Duncan and I chatted and agreed to run together again. We'd felt it had gone well up until his nosebleed, and thought we could both do with the company, and balancing influence of the other.

Before long, the night began to fade, and I took the opportunity to visit the little boy's room. I walked away from the camp, and as I did so, I walked into one of the most surprising, yet in my eyes, heart-warming encounters of my time in the desert. There, sat on the ground, was a runner who was contentedly puffing on a cigarette. I couldn't believe it. In an event that is based on fitness and packing absolute bare minimum supplies, here was a guy who was not only smoking, but carrying his fags with him all week! He was probably late-40s, thin and sinewy like a whippet, and in my estimation either in the forces, or ex-forces. I strolled over to him. He spoke in a gravelly Scottish accent, a bit like Begbie out of Trainspotting.

Me: 'How's it going buddy?'

Him: 'Good mate, and how's you?'

Me: 'Yeah, I'm ok. Had a better day today. Have you had a good day?'

Him: 'Yeah, ok. I'm not looking to break any records. I just always wanted to tick this one off the list.'

BIG DRAG ON FAG

Me: 'Good for you mate. I'm the same. Got to get these things ticked off. Do you mind if I ask you something?'

Him: 'Course not mate.... [Laughs....]'

Me: 'How many of those are you getting through whilst you're out here?'

Him: '20. I bought a pack of 20. I'm having 3 a day other than the last day when I'll have 2.'

Me: 'Do you know what...'

Him: 'You think I'm a twat, ey?'

Me: 'Not in the slightest. I wasn't going to say that...'

I smiled as I said it, and I think he realised I wasn't criticising him, but almost more in awe...

Him: 'Listen, I'm not here to win the fuckin' thing, and I don't do this running caper because I'm dreaming of being on the front of Men's Health. I do this because this shit, experiencing life... it makes my fucking dick hard. I'm addicted to it. I've seen me mates fuckin' blown up in front of me, fuckin' turned into red mist, standing on a fuckin' landmine. I do this because it makes me feel alive.'

Me: 'I think I can understand that. I don't think you're a twat at all. I'm doing this because I worry that one day I'll run out of time to do all the things I want to do. I actually think it's pretty fucking cool to see such barefaced normality right here in the middle of all this nonsense. 75 yards away there are people sat in the Lotus position, chugging recovery shakes, macadamia nuts and isotonic gels, and here you are sucking on a B&H. Happy days.'

Him: 'Marlboro Light, pal.'

Me: 'What?'

Him: 'I'm smoking Marlboro Lights, no B&H. I'm not a complete fuckin' idiot.'

And with that, he laughed and walked off; and I never saw him again.

To many reading this, it may seem appalling that someone would smoke mid-MDS. And I guess it is, but from my standpoint, I actually thought, and still do think, that it was fantastic. The legend and the myth of the MDS can overtake things, and it is in the interests of the organisers for this to continue. They pedal it; of course they do. But this was a perfect encapsulation of how the people out there on the course aren't superhuman. They're just regular people, with regular lives, who choose to try to tackle an extraordinary challenge.

I returned from my toilet trip and bowled into our tent. 'There's a bloke over there, fucking smoking!' Everyone reacted the same as me. Incredulous, but amused. We all lay there laughing for a good while about our smoking friend. At this point, Jules announced that he'd brought a little bottle of spiced rum with him for a celebratory tipple at the finish line. Again, I loved the normality of it.

The cigarette and the rum points to an important characteristic of the MDS. Of course, it is a huge physical challenge. But it's not the physical side of things that sets most of the competitors apart from the 'average bear.' It's the mental side of things. First and foremost, the people out there are willing to take on the challenge, and mad enough to think they may be able to do it. And in taking it on, they're willing to accept the possibility of failure. Granted, there are some exceptionally fit specimens within the bivouac, but beyond that there are all sorts of shapes and sizes. You may be able to see that they have a little bit of excess weight around their middle, but what you can't see, is what they have between the ears. Since returning, I've lost count of the amount of times I have said to someone *'trust me, if you wanted to, you could do the MDS... you just need to approach it positively.'* And if you try, and fail... so what? Failure, after all, is the privilege of those with the guts to try.

When I was a kid and running competitively, there was a lad who was a year older than me. I ran for Coventry and he ran for Solihull. He was head and shoulders above the rest of us ability wise. He had an England vest and I couldn't get anywhere near him; he was just far too quick over anything between a mile and 5k. One day though, I was racing him in a team road relay event at Sutton Park, and I managed to stick with him until around half way, on the 5k course. He suddenly started screaming; literally bawling out to his supporters at the side of the route. 'I've got a stich. I'VE GOT A STICH!!' This continued for about 500m, and I took the opportunity to inject a bit more pace. At this point, he literally burst into tears and walked to the edge of the course, binning not only his race, but that of his entire team, who needed him to 'get the baton round.' It turned out, he could only win, and in fact, only run, if he was miles ahead. He didn't have it between the ears. It sounds harsh to judge, but he's exactly the sort of guy who would struggle at the MDS. Unlike the steady plodder who takes the pain, takes the knocks, looks for the positives, gets up whenever they fall down and goes again. Someone once said to me 'an average runner with a great mindset will do better at the MDS than a great runner with an average mindset.' I think this is pretty much spot on.

This is why, if you think you can do the MDS, the reality is, you quite probably can.

That night, our emails came in. I received around 20 messages from home, which prompted some light-hearted mock jealousy from my tent mates. In the collection of messages were the usual ones from my family, and also some messages from people I would never have expected to take time out of their day. It was genuinely humbling, and really did spur me on to new levels of motivation. I'd publicised that I was doing the MDS a lot on social media, in order to both generate sponsorship and also support. Even so, I was shocked by some of messages I received. It appeared that the event had really captured people's imagination, and they were avidly tracking my progress. I saved the messages from Lucy, Millie and Ted until last. After I read them, Jules caught me by my shoulder and said 'are you ok Nellie?' I said I was and asked why. He said 'because you've been staring blankly into space for ages.' I chuckled and explained that Millie's note, and her customary 'I just know you can do it, daddy' had caught a heart-string. Others in the tent read out some of their messages, and we all enjoyed the support each of us was getting from back home. Paul, who had originally introduced me to the group that made up Tent 143 was expecting twins. They weren't due imminently but being twins there was a chance they could come early. We all therefore took particular interest in his communication with home. As of yet, there was no news.

We all climbed into our respective beds, and got our heads down. We were awoken sharply by a vicious storm. Our tent was blowing all over the place, and without warning, the main pole in the middle came crashing down. It landed between me and Jorge, with no damage done. That said, we were now all pretty much lying under one massive blanket, with sand blowing into our faces at pretty high force. I later found out that Jules and Duncan had sat up for ages, trying to prop the tent up, but had eventually given in and lay down with the tent resting on their faces. Seemingly, just as suddenly as the wind whipped up, the berbers were on hand, re-constructing our tent, and securing it in a more sturdy fashion. Our fatigue meant that we all fell back to sleep very quickly. Whilst annoyed at the interruption, I was actually quite glad that it had happened. It was another element to feeling that I was experiencing the 'full Sahara package.'

CHAPTER 14

Day 3 – 31.6km

I woke up to find I had sand in my ears, my nose and in my mouth. It was horrible. The sand wasn't like the sort of sand you encounter on the beach, where it is quite gritty. This sand was much finer; almost like a dust. Up until this point, the sand hadn't really bothered me, however this felt almost suffocating in its ability to get into every last nook and cranny. I stuck my finger in my ear and pulled it out. It was coated. Fortunately I had packed with me some Wemmi Wipes. These are fantastic little things, and a definite 'must have' in the desert. They are dehydrated wet wipes that are compacted to around the size of a polo mint. You drop a tiny amount of water onto them and they expand and turn into very effective means of cleaning your face. *When I say 'effective,' it is all relative to the situation!*

We all began to rise up out of our sleeping bags, and there was instant laughter. The inside of our tent looked no different to the outside of the tent. You couldn't see the mat on the floor because it was entirely covered with sand; as was nearly all of our belongings. The wind had long since died down, so we began shaking and dusting our possessions down as best we could, before the standard morning ritual of teeth brushing, breakfast cooking and general body preparation for the day ahead.

Once I was up and walking around, the first thing I noticed wasn't my toes, which had been my primary concern, but my shoulder. The pressure point that had become apparent right at the start of the first day had been getting steadily worse. I'd tried various tactics to cushion this element of my strap, including using my down jacket as padding, using some spare socks, and finally using my flip-flop. They had all offered up some small relief, but thus far it had not actually hurt before I put my pack on. This morning, it was sore to the touch and I couldn't put any pressure on it without wincing in pain. I had been hoping that the progressively lighter pack, as we proceeded through the days, would mean that the problem would become less of an issue, but I had clearly been being either naïve or just unrealistically optimistic.

I decided to strap my spare socks over the offending area, and also modify my flip-flops to be able to tie them to the straps of my backpack. This involved cutting the 'thong' section that goes between your toes, and rendering them pretty much useless as footwear. I didn't care. I could cope without flip-flops of an evening. But if I didn't sort this issue with my pack, I was going to struggle to keep on going. I carried out all of the modifications, ably assisted by my tent friends. As we were doing so, a fellow runner who I'd hitherto never set eyes on before walked up to me and said 'Are you using the Salomon pack?' I told him that I was and he said that he was too and that was having the exact same issue as me. In fact, he said he'd seen a handful of people on the course with the pack, and that everyone was suffering due to the same issue.

I had gone with the Salomon pack due to a variety of positive reviews that I had read. The pack has a 'vest' rather than strap design, which is supposed to make it more comfortable. It also has a variety of draw-strings that are used to both tighten the pack to your body, and also shrink the overall pack size as its contents reduce throughout the race. The problem was being caused by a hard plastic junction box within the shoulder section of the strap. This box connected a few different draw-strings. As such there was considerable pressure on the box, and the physics of the design meant that it was being pulled down hard, just below my clavicle. I trained with the pack a lot before leaving England – probably approximately 200 miles worth of running. I have never understood how the problem hadn't surfaced before my arrival at the desert, but I had definitely chosen the wrong pack for my bodyshape.

It was bitterly cold that third morning. This wasn't a problem. It just meant that we all kept our down-jackets on until the last minute. By this point, we were too switched on to the nuances of the desert to think that a colder morning may mean a cooler midday; it just doesn't work like that! It was around this time that the bond and the camaraderie between us as a group had really taken hold. We'd just endured a sandstorm together, and had slept rubbing shoulders for a few nights now. We'd shared some life stories; probably telling each other details about our lives that we haven't told very close friends back home. More importantly we had all completed 2 out of the 7 days; we knew we could run in the desert. And this meant that we were all getting closer to our dream. But the closer you get, the more you fear it being taken away. Each of us had different drivers for being out there, but ultimately we all had the same collective goal, and that was bonding us.

In the back of our minds, we all had the following day. ***The Long Day.*** There were mutterings to each other as we assembled at the start. 'Don't do anything stupid today.' 'Make sure you leave plenty in the tank for tomorrow.' 'Nice and steady folks, nice and steady.' Patrick Bauer took his customary position on the top of his Land Rover, microphone in hand. His opening line was delivered with comedy timing perfection. 'Welcome to Morocco. Sorry about the wind.' Everyone fell about laughing. Patrick, explained that today was going to be a tough day, course wise. We had read as much in the course map, but had hoped it was an exaggeration. They wouldn't give us a really tough day, the day before the Long Day, would they? Well yes, evidently they would!

The familiar strains of ACDC fired up, Patrick did his countdown, and we were off.

Instantly, I knew I was in trouble with my shoulder. I put my hand underneath it to try to relieve the pressure, which helped a bit, but not enough. As I ran, I considered whether I could run holding my bag in front of me, rather than strapping it to my back. We ran on for a few miles, and Duncan noticed that I was unusually quiet. I explained my predicament to him and asked if he could fish my down-jacket out of my pack. He did that and I stuffed it under my strap, and we continued. Despite this third layer of padding, my shoulder continued to cause me serious discomfort, and I began to seriously consider the idea of taking my pack off and carrying it in front of me. At this point however, I happened to run up alongside a lad I had met at the Pilgrims event back in the UK. He asked how I was and when I told him my situation, he fished out a small pack of tiny tablets. 'Here you go buddy; take some of these,' he said. I asked him what they were and he explained that they were seriously powerful codeine tablets that he had 'acquired off his mate, a dentist.' After he confirmed that he definitely had enough to spare me some, I gratefully took a few of them and put them into my salt-tablet bag – being sure to check that they were obviously different in shape and size to the salt tablets!

Duncan and I ran on and had a mini debate about these tablets. Up until now, I hadn't taken any painkillers at all, and I was reluctant to do so, but was starting to think that I had no choice. The debate was pretty short and went along these lines:

Me: 'Do you know much about codeine?'
Duncan: 'Powerful painkiller.'

Me: 'Yeah, that's about what I know. Any side-effects that you know of? All I know of is it can make you a bit woozey, and also make you constipated.'

Duncan: 'That's about all I know to be honest mate.'

Me: 'I can live with both of those. I'll take one. If I fall off the edge of a jebel, could you let an official know?'

Much laugher ensued between us and I opened up my little bag.

Me: 'FUCK!!!'

Duncan: 'What's the matter mate?'

Me: 'I've just taken two by mistake!!'

Duncan: 'Really?! [laughs] Well, I wouldn't worry about feeling your pack, pretty soon you're not going to feel anything at all!'

Having doubled up on the painkillers I was now concerned that they were going to make me vomit. As it was, however, I experienced no side-effects at all, other than the pain in my shoulder numbing to an acceptable level within around 15 minutes. On we went.

Day 3 had started hard. Very soon after the start, we headed into sand dunes which were incredibly energy sapping. It worked both your aerobic and anaerobic fitness, and again I was thankful for the combination of gym work and road work I had done as part of my training. Duncan and I had agreed between us that we were going to take the day very steady, so we were intentionally keeping the brakes on a touch to start off with. The benefit of doing this, and of remaining mid-pack within the race, is that there are always people around you, and always people to follow. This means you can very easily see the terrain that lies ahead of you. The runners in front stretch out like a line of ants. After the dunes, the ground underfoot became firmer and the elevation gradually began to increase. The terrain became more and more rocky, and then we took a left hand turn behind some large rocks that had up until this point shielded our view of what was to come. As we turned, the view opened up to reveal an extremely steep climb ahead of us. So steep, in fact, that there appeared to be a rope set out to allow runners to haul themselves up. 'You seen that?' I said to Duncan. 'Oh goody,' came his response, laced with a combination of irony and amusement. As he said this, we overtook a few people and one of them shouted 'Hey, it's the two Duncans – keep going guys!!' We didn't think much of it and carried on.

The terrain became very tricky at this point, and we all had to travel single file in order to pick our way through the rocks. After a short time I became aware of a pretty rank smell. I didn't give it much thought. We were all eating fairly strange concoctions whilst out there so the occasional unpleasant smell wasn't particularly newsworthy. After about 10 minutes, this one still hadn't gone away though. I was picking my way through the rocks, head down, thinking to myself 'how in all that is holy has someone eaten such total muck as to make the entire Sahara Desert smell bad?!' I then looked up to see a chap, about 3 or 4 people ahead of me, swinging a heavily laden poo bag by his side. You had to be kidding me?! By this point, everyone behind him had cottoned on. There were a few other Brits nearby who started calling out 'what the heck is that smell mate? Jesus, can't you do something with it?!' 10 or so minutes later the terrain opened up a touch and we all made a mad dash to overtake him. As we went past, Duncan said to him 'mate, wouldn't it be a good idea to bury that, or at least tie a knot in it?' As clear as day, the chap said 'no, I am alright thanks. I think I'll just keep going as I am.' We scurried off, mouthing 'what the fuck?!' at each other.

The next 3 hours remain one of the most vivid memories that I have of the entire week in the desert. We climbed another very steep ascent that required a rope to help us on our way. At times it was actually pretty dangerous and you had to be extremely sure of your footing due to the size of the boulders you were climbing up. Each 'step' was probably a foot in height, with precious little surface area for purchase. When we reached the top we ran along the spine of a ridgeway. The view suddenly opened out and no matter which way you looked, it was astonishing. The closest I can compare it to is the Grand Canyon. It appeared that we were running along a ridge that separated two huge bowls; one each side. To the far left there were jebels, and the same to the far right. I later learned that we were running along what was once a sea bed. I stopped for a few seconds to take a few pictures on my phone, before returning to my trot.

The combination of the baron landscape, the jebels in the distance, the cloudless sky, and the line of runners trying to 'beat the desert' through sheer force of will rendered me awe-struck. Despite all of the pain and discomfort, right here, right now, I was having the time of my life. Human endeavor has always fascinated me. Whether it's Usain Bolt running a 100m quicker than anyone ever thought possible, Sir Edmund Hillary ascending Everest, or regular people pushing themselves to their limit, I love seeing what the human mind and body can achieve. At this precise moment in time, I was quite literally a living breathing cog in the wheel of human spirit vs nature. And I loved it. There have been certain moments in my life that I know I'll never forget. There are the obvious ones; the births, the deaths, the weddings, the drunken pub crawl skiing down a mountain in the pitch black, but this was right up there.

The course banked off to the left before dropping down sharply with a steep downhill section. Excitingly however, this downhill was in extremely deep, extremely soft sand. What this meant was, we could sprint, full-tilt down the section without any danger of being hurt if we fell. It was like a mini-adventure playground for runners! As we reached the bottom, we looked up to see that we were about to run the full width of the bowl, which I assume was originally a sea bay until we reached the jebels on the other side. I shouted to Duncan 'how far do you reckon that is mate?' He shouted back, 'well, it's got to be further than it looks.' Between us, we decided it was about 2 miles, and that we'd aim to run it all without any walking or rest.

For anyone who isn't up to speed, and in case I haven't made it clear already; there is a hell of a lot of walking involved in the MDS. The elite runners may run most of the way, but the vast majority of 'runners' are actually either 'run-walkers' or even out and out 'walkers.' My approach (and Duncan's) was to run for a bit, and walk for a bit. There was no exact science. Some people rigorously applied a run for 5 minutes, walk for 10 minutes approach. For others it was a case of run anything that is flat or downhill, and walk everything that is uphill; no matter how shallow the gradient. For us, it was all down to how we felt at the time. 'Do you mind if we walk for a bit mate?' Or 'fancy having a little trot for a while?' It worked well for us. I think at times we probably both encouraged each other to run when we didn't want to, but also to walk when we felt we could have run. Overall, it worked well to conserve and maintain our energy levels.

We ran on into the 'bowl.' The heat had taken a notch up now, but the landscape was remarkable. It was akin to the videos I have seen of the salt plains out in Oklahoma. It was very useful to have such a neatly bookended section of the run. There was no debate about what the next landmark to aim for was. Out there in the distance was a very obvious jebel. We were running to that; no stopping, no walking. It was just 2 miles away...

Only it wasn't 2 miles away... 2 miles came and went, and the jebel was barely any closer. We got to 3 miles and it looked like we were around about half way. We decided we'd walk for a minute to conserve some energy and also get some fuel on board. This was a real blow to me mentally. I'd told myself that I was going to run the full width of the bowl and now I was 'wimping out.' I was trying to wrestle with inner demons. I knew I was being ridiculous. This was a self-imposed target; it really didn't matter whether I hit it or not, but I hate not hitting targets whoever has set them. As ridiculous as it sounds, during the minute or so that we walked, I had to keep telling myself that I was walking, not because I had to – not because I couldn't run to the jebel, but because it was the sensible thing to do. In many ways, the MDS is an exercise in management; managing your nutrition, your feet, your kit, your body, and your mind. This was just one example of that. Soon enough though, we were up and running again and I pushed all negative thoughts to the back of my mind and kept moving forward.

It turned out the bowl itself was a little over 5 miles. That we initially thought it was around 2 miles only goes to show how much the landscape in the desert can mess with your sense of perspective. When we eventually reached the other side, we proceeded to take on the incline that took us out of the valley. This meant walking, which was a very welcome break as by this point the temperature had really started to heat up. We climbed the side of the jebel and then descended the other side. I saw Ian Corless who is an official photographer, and well known on the circuit. It was strangely comforting, seeing Ian. He doesn't know me from Adam, but seeing him gave me an almost palpable sense of reassurance. We pushed on and discussed what was likely to be coming up on the course. We knew that there was to be a testing section, but I was feeling pretty good so was actually quite excited. How wrong I was!

We approached the jebel and it was both steep and tricky underfoot. It was sufficiently precarious that they had set out a rope to pull yourself up. It was agony on the quads. It also meant that you could quite easily become stuck in a 'traffic jam.' This wasn't overly bad news, but a little frustrating at times. In terms of gradient, it was effectively like climbing a step ladder, in parts; yet not so uniformed and easily approached. I was quite taken aback as I hadn't expected this level of technicality to the course. Eventually we reached the summit and then began our descent. This was even worse!

I realised when doing day 2 of the Pilgrims Ultra, and running down precarious, slippery steps, that my technical abilities are pretty poor. What would typically happen is other runners would overtake me on the downhill, and I would catch them up on the flat and uphill sections. I don't really understand why I was / am so poor at running down the technical sections, but I most definitely am. It seems a bit like skiing where other people can happily attack mogul fields whilst I tentatively try to pick my way down without avoiding injury. To give you an idea of the terrain we were now facing, whilst running down the other side to the jebel we had just run up, the gradient was probably a negative 1 in 10, and the ground itself was littered with rocks; all of which were at least the size of a good sized family suitcase. By this point, we were roughly two thirds of the way into the day's course, and had just tackled the ascent so were reasonably fatigued. Concentration was absolutely critical to avoid rolling an ankle. I became paranoid; it would be devastating to have to abandon the race not because you weren't fit enough, but because you'd injured yourself. As irrational as it sounds, I started to get really quite angry with the course markers! I was carefully navigating a path through the rock debris muttering to myself, 'well this is just fucking irresponsible, making us run through this! How stupid!'

I became aware of people behind me, pretty much clipping my heels. This is always a difficult dynamic to deal with. It's mentally tough to deal with on a few different levels. I was annoyed that I wasn't going faster than I was. I was anxious because I didn't want to injure myself. I felt a sense of guilt that I was holding other people up. I felt a sense of shame *because* I was holding other people up. And finally, I was getting angry that the person who was quite literally clipping my heels was increasing my chances of injury. Even writing it now I can feel a slight quickening of my pulse as I remember how cross it had made me. After a minute or so, hoping they spoke English, I shouted 'do you want to go past?' The chap replied 'no, you're alright mate.' So I took matters into my own hands and ran off to the side to force him to overtake me. I then ran down the edge of this section of the course, and watched as approximately 20 people ran past. This tricky downhill section lasted approximately 2km before levelling out and turning into full on sand dunes. By this point, I was really feeling the heat. Duncan and I were back running side by side and we stopped to get some water on board. Having taken the extra bottle at the previous checkpoint, I had sufficient to pour some over my head. This was tough. I'd gone from feeling very good, to very weak within an hour. This isn't particularly surprising, and it's always important to remember with long distant running that you will go through bad patches and good patches. But they are just that; patches. Nothing lasts forever.

Duncan told me he was feeling similar to me, so we made the decision to walk all of the soft sand. We didn't know how long this would last, but it gave us a chance to talk and re-gather our thoughts. As we walked, we spotted some of the officials blasting over the dunes in a Kawasaki Mule. The contrast in their emotions vs ours could not have been more stark. How much I wanted to ask them for a lift! It is incredibly tiring climbing a sand dune. Every time you put your foot into the sand, it goes so deep that you barely make any progress at all. I suspect you end up taking 3 or 4 strides for every one that you would take on a similar incline that featured hardstanding. The sand itself will cover your foot entirely, and rise to roughly half way up your shin. As tiring as it was though, and as tired as *I was*, I couldn't help but marvel at the beauty and power of nature. We pushed on, and after another 2km or so, the ground firmed up and we were back to our trot.

Discussion turned to the following day; the long day. We knew that we were now entering the final stages of Day 3, so all tactics were based around entering the long day as fresh as possible. 'Let's walk for a bit,' Duncan said. I gratefully agreed, which was useful because at precisely this moment, we went up a slight incline and found ourselves on a flat plain that was like being in a wind tunnel. This was to be our run in to the finish. The wind was vicious and energy sapping. It also hurt! Sand was being blown into our faces. I was thankful that I had spent quite some time researching my glasses, and had a pair with a foam liner that effectively sealed them to my face, preventing any sand from getting near my eyes.

I found this section tough. There's no denying that it was difficult, but a contributory factor in my emotion was definitely the following day looming in the background. The truth is, I was having to 'grind it out' more than I would have wanted at this stage. The combination of the wind and the heat meant it was a case of putting your head down and pushing on; there wasn't a lot of enjoyment at this stage! As we went, we overtook a few people, while a few other people overtook us. It barely registered. This wasn't about placings, but getting the day ticked off and getting our feet up. After approximately an hour I caught sight of the inflatable gantry that makes up the finish line. It was still roughly one mile away, and we elected to pick up the pace. The course skirted from right to left, and was then a straight run into the finish. It was both eerie and romantic. Ahead of us was totally baron, apart from one person, kicking up dust, who was just as stupid as we were. Watching this person run in, was quite inspiring for me. Whilst we were doing exactly the same as him / her, I felt privileged to have such an intimate view of this human vs nature battle. The solitude and basic nature of the struggle is what had interested me in the first place. Watching this person getting ever closer to the finish line, and wondering what inner-voice was driving them on inspired me.

Three or four minutes later Duncan and I crossed the line. I finished in 420th place in 5hr30m. Him one second ahead of me in 419th position. We drank our tea gratefully, gathered our water and headed to the tent. The next few hours are strange within my memory and brain.

I've always been a fairly intense person. An ability and willingness to single-mindedly pursue something at any cost is both a strength and a weakness. I will typically mentally decide I'm doing something, without checking with anyone or anything, and assume that I will be able to put in place the necessary mechanisms to make it happen. The end goal becomes all consuming, and there can be quite a lot of collateral damage, if I'm not careful. It is difficult to describe, but it is like mentally, my view of the world becomes increasingly narrow until ultimately all I can see is a direct path to the goal I am focused on. This has happened on a number of occasions, in both work and pleasure. From business deals to sub-3 hour marathons, the behavioural pattern is a well-trodden path. Whilst it can serve me well, it can also cause me problems, and ultimately, it is not something I am particularly proud of as invariably, when I enter this frame of mind my mood turns fairly dark, extremely selfish and I become moody and impatient. Whilst I didn't realise it at the time, looking back it is clear that having finished Day 3, I was now entering this state of mind.

I remember precious little about the evening of Day 3. I couldn't even tell you what order we arrived back at our tent in, although I was ecstatic that again we finished with a full complement. The mood in the camp was edgy; it was the calm before the storm. That night, letters were delivered to the camp, and I know that I sent an email home. It is almost like my body gave up on making memories, though, in order to preserve energy for the day to come. I can tell you nothing about the content of any of the communications, nor any conversations with team mates before bed.

CHAPTER 15

Day 4 – 86.2 km.

The Long Day

"Today; we die a little" -
Emile Zatopek

awoke at just after 5am. My emotions were mixed. In many ways I was dreading what was to come, but equally, I was excited and relieved that this day was finally here. Ever since I had first read of the MDS back in 1998, it was the Long Day that had captured my imagination and then gone on to cause me such angst. A double marathon. Carrying all of your kit. Running through sand. In blistering heat. I'd spent hours pounding the streets, pounding my treadmill, and more recently sitting in saunas, and then running on my treadmill surrounded by heaters. It had all been about this.

I've always had a theory that once you've got past the stage of the challenge no longer being merely completing a marathon, but of what time you do it in, your training takes on a different dynamic. You aren't really training for a marathon; you're training for a 10km. But the 10km in question will be run following 20 miles. That's similar to how I felt about the MDS. You were training for a week's worth of ultra-running, but in reality, you were training for this one very specific day. The thought that within 24 hours, I'd know the answer to my question of myself was both terrifying and wonderfully exciting.

The mood in the camp was difficult to describe. There was an awful lot of pent up energy; a combination of excitement and fear. I guess a lot of people were feeling exactly the same as me. I paid extra attention to my organisation. I wanted to ensure that I had everything ready to hand. This meant stuffing my bumbag with 6 energy gels that I had been saving for this day, along with a Cliff bar and some Haribo. My plan was to try to get by without them, but if I needed them to get through the day, I would eat them without a second thought.

The Long Day at the MDS is actually two days. The rules are that you must complete a double marathon by roughly dusk the day after the morning you set off. Some people have a plan from the outset to stop for a rest half way. Some will actually sleep. Others choose to stop to make a cooked meal. My plan was, and had always been, to try to do it non-stop. This was driven by both rational and emotional factors. Rationally, it actually makes more sense to do it in one go as it means you have longer to recover. Whilst the people at the front, zipping round in next to no time are impressive, the people at the back, taking close to 36 hours to complete the same course deserve as much, if not more applause. They are putting their bodies through a much tougher ordeal. I, for one, wanted to try to get it done as soon as possible.

Emotionally, I was also wedded to the idea of doing it in one go. Ever since my dad had died, I had always worried that I'd not grieved properly. Timings and life hadn't really allowed it. First I had to take over the running of the family business, and then I'd become a new father myself. These two things had meant I'd been on a constant hamster wheel, and never been able to break things down in my head. As strange as it may sound, I'd long earmarked this double marathon as being a cathartic exercise in my life. I knew it was going to strip me back bare, and was actually relishing this. I wanted to be pushed to my absolute limit. I wanted to be put into a place where I thought I was on the brink. I was looking forward to stripping everything away; no outside world... No work, no family, no friends. Just me. Me against me. Let's see what you're made of, big boy.

Mentally, I had set myself a target of 20 hours. Having examined previous years' results, I felt finishing in 20 hours would be a very positive result. But this was a distant second target behind the principal aim of finishing at all.

Duncan and I got our heads together as we made final preparations to our packs. 'Get the job done,' was our mantra. No heroics; no risking going too fast. Just a case of slow and steady, one foot in front of the other. We also had a conversation about what we would do if one of us ran into problems. This maybe seems an unnecessary conversation, as ultimately, the one not suffering would obviously go ahead alone, but we had become extremely close in our pursuit of our shared goal, and it felt appropriate to at least have the conversation.

I still had my flip-flops attached under the straps of my backpack, and my right shoulder was now extremely sore, but beyond the stage of acute pain, and more like a very deep, dull pain. I was sure that the flip-flops were essential to being able to make it through the day. Tent 143 all gathered together briefly before we headed off to the start line. There were no speeches nor rallying cries. Just a relatively short moment of intimate understanding, emotional connection and goodwill. We all knew that this was our Everest. Finish the Long Day, and in all likelihood, we'd complete the Marathon Des Sables 2018. 'Go well, team,' I said as we all disbanded to make our way to the start. I said it as much to myself as to anyone else.

We gathered on the start line and Patrick began his customary announcement. Unsurprisingly, given this was the long day, so too his address lasted an inordinately long time! He explained that today was going to be the hottest day so far (perfect) and that the course for the stage was not without its challenges (even better). He wished us well, fired up 'Highway to Hell' and then the countdown began. 'Trois, deux, un.... GO!' We started off extremely steady; walking in fact. We'd decided that we would ease ourselves into the day very gradually and may even walk the first 5km without exception. As it was, we soon began to get restless and broke into a very slow run.

The early part of the course saw us run through a very small village. The houses are effectively mud-huts, with donkeys tied up outside. This is evidently an extremely simple way of life however the children outside could not have appeared happier. They were excitedly waving and cheering every runner who went past. I found it humbling to think of the lives of these children versus my own kids and gladly high-fived a few as I went past. As we continued, we saw a sign for a

Holiday Park. You could hear murmurs of amusement amongst the pack as we ran past it. 'Don't think I could convince the family to come here for next year's summer holiday!' was the general gist. By this point, we were roughly 10km in, and alternating between a slow run, and a fast march. The sun had come out in full force, and it was heating up to an uncomfortable extent, despite being only a little after 10am.

My backpack began to weigh heavy on my shoulders. (In actual fact, it was feeling pretty light after I'd eaten 3 days' worth of supplies). I didn't worry however. Pain in my shoulders wasn't going to stop me. It wasn't *able* to stop me; not in the way that ruined feet could. Worst case, I'd still got some of the codeine tablets I had been given, if the pain became unbearable later in the day. I didn't say anything to Duncan as I wanted us to be as positive as possible given the day ahead. The course was easy underfoot at this stage, with firm ground. We got to the first checkpoint in 2hr7m and felt both felt reasonable. We were religiously taking our salt tablets that were provided by the organisers, but put even more effort in on this day. I'm a heavy sweater when I run at the best of times, so given the marked difference in heat on Day 4, I took 3 tablets for every one bottle, rather than the 2 per bottle I had hitherto been going with.

We pushed through the checkpoint and made relatively easy work of the next section, arriving at checkpoint 2 in 4hr15m. The temperature was now very, very hot. I think afterwards there were reports of it hitting around 48c, which isn't as hot as some previous years, but was still very uncomfortable. The air that you're breathing is hot. It therefore feels like you're heating your body up from the inside with every breath. I had assumed that I would be drenched in sweat but the reality when you are out there is that you are very dry. It is not that you're not sweating; far from it in fact. You are sweating litres and litres of fluid each day, but the extreme heat means it evaporates instantly.

We spent a few minutes at checkpoint 2, sheltering in some shade under one of the open sided tents. We gratefully chugged down some water, but we only had 1.5L until the next checkpoint when we would be given a further 3L. The second I stepped out of the shade, the heat was oppressive, and the sheer power of the sun was something to behold. I had opted for a long sleeve top for the week, which offers total sunblock. In addition I was wearing long socks and a cap with a neck flap. As such, very little of my skin was on show, and any that was had been swathed in total sunblock. I wasn't going to burn, but this didn't change the incredible power within the rays of the sun. The closest I can remember enduring was on a trip to Las Vegas when I felt unable to stay out in the sun for any longer than a few minutes. Here, I was going to have to run in it all day!

We set off again, however we were noticeably slower on our feet. A lot of people had said that they intended to walk throughout the 'heat of the day' hours. We were keen to keep running for as long as we could so we put our heads down and looked to cover some ground in intensive bursts. I remember the following 5km of the day extraordinarily clearly. Duncan and I had drifted into our own personal mental spaces and weren't talking much. It wasn't like we'd fallen out, but were having to focus our energies on the task in hand. Around this time, I started to build up the occasional lead ahead of Duncan. Nothing major; probably around 50-60 metres. I would turn back to nod some approval and realise he was a bit behind, so slow down to allow him to catch me up. It happened probably 3 or 4 times. The temperature had seemingly increased again and I felt very exposed. I found myself subconsciously looking at the route ahead of me to see if I could spot any areas of shade to travel through. On the whole, there was nothing, however after a while, I did notice an area ahead with approximately 10 – 15 trees disparately spread. I changed my direction slightly to take these in. I looked back and saw Duncan quite a way back, and talked with a fellow Brit whilst travelling more slowly to allow my partner in crime to catch up.

When Duncan did get to me, he was behaving a little strangely. He was very distant and unusually downbeat. My attempts at jollying him along fell on deaf ears. My watch suggested we were around 5km from the next checkpoint. 'I'm really struggling, mate,' Duncan said. 'You'll be fine big man. We'll just go nice and slow, and then we can have ourselves a wee rest at the checkpoint. Keep it going; no pressure.' I could see that Duncan was in trouble but was confident that we could sort it at the next checkpoint. I asked him to go in front of me so that I could stay in close contact. The three miles to the checkpoint were purgatory. I tried to keep offering up words of encouragement to Duncan, but I think in reality, they were also aimed at myself. 'Not long to go now big boy. Let's just get to the next water stop and regroup.' My behaviour was actually reminiscent of how my 6 year old daughter comforts her 3 year old brother. 'Don't worry Teddy, mummy and daddy will be home soon.' She's saying it to herself as much as she is him – and here, I was doing the same thing!

The run up to the third checkpoint saw us begin a relatively steady incline on a totally exposed section of the course. This was so extremely tough. Having said that the sweat typically evaporates as soon as you produce it, despite the extreme heat, I was becoming noticeably sweaty. I was starting to get a little concerned about my fluid levels. I hadn't been for a wee for a while, which wasn't the best sign. I gave my bottles a quick shake and had precious little fluid left. Thankfully, at this point the checkpoint came into view. It was approximately 800m ahead so I greedily drank down the fluid I had left. We got into the checkpoint in a little under 7 hours and took our 3 litres of water. I was a little spooked by the fact that I had effectively run out of water in the run up to this check point. I reminded myself that this wasn't just a footrace but also a potential danger to my health. I vowed to redouble my efforts to manage all of my admin better.

After taking my water, I looked around but had lost eyes on Duncan. I had a quick wander around but still couldn't find him.

Eventually I heard him call out; he was sitting in one of the tents. I went in and sat down next to him. Sitting down wasn't quite as easy as it sounds and involved taking my pack of which had a variety of straps and strings, and then folding my legs down which were unsurprisingly rather stiff! I sat down next to Duncan who was looking in very poor shape. I gave his leg a supportive 'tap,' and left him to it for a bit. We both needed some time to gather ourselves and get some fluid and food on board. After about 10 minutes, I asked Duncan how he was feeling. He was verging on incoherent and said he felt he should see the doctor. I advised him to hang fire and see how he felt in a few minutes time. These minutes came and went and he repeated his wish to see the doctor. I was petrified that a doctor may look at him and pull him out, so again said 'mate, let's just give it a few more minutes.' When he said it a third time, I came to my senses and stopped trying to involve myself in decisions that weren't mine to take – no matter how well intended I thought my actions were.

Duncan saw the doctor who gave him some dioralyhte and told him to focus on getting his fluids back to normal levels. He was extremely dehydrated. He sat back down next to me and told me to go on alone. I told him I wasn't prepared to do this, and asked him how long he felt he needed to get himself back together. He said 'about an hour,' and I agreed without hesitation. Duncan seemed uncomfortable with this, but in my eyes, he'd helped me when I had so needed it on Day 2, after my tough first day. I wanted to repay the favour. And to be honest, the rest wasn't totally unwelcome. We sat in silence and ate some fuel. I had packed some fruit and nut mix and this came in handy. After a bit, Duncan lay down and I followed suit. I didn't want him to feel that I was straining at the leash, and also thought it would be of benefit to me if I could get my legs up above my heart.

The prescribed hour came and went in the blink of an eye. During this time literally hundreds of runners came through the checkpoint and leapfrogged us. This was of no concern whatsoever. I asked Duncan how he was feeling and he replied that he was still suffering and repeated his desire for me to go on without him. I said I'd wait. A further 10 minutes went by and Duncan started making noises that he was worried about whether he may be able to beat the cut off periods that are in place. This concerned me a great deal and I started to consider the option I had been trying to put to the back of my mind. If he was feeling that bad, I may have to go on alone to avoid us both missing a cut off. We talked things through. I said we'd wait another 15 minutes or so and take a view. Duncan implored me to leave already, but I felt almost physically attached to him. When this time came and went, Duncan made my decision for me, telling me politely but firmly that I was to leave. I was racked with guilt. How could I leave, not knowing what was going to happen to Duncan, who had been so integral to my journey thus far. Whilst a more understated character than me, this meant every bit as much to him as it did me. I must have asked 'are you sure' ten or more times before I put my back pack on. When the weight of my pack went on, however, I winced in pain as my shoulders felt bruised. I had an epiphanal moment however when I realised it was the hard undersole of my flip-flops pushing down on my shoulders that had caused this. I took my pack back off and removed my flip-flops from the straps before putting it back on and securing all of the loops and straps. I went into the tent and said an emotional (from my point of view) goodbye to Duncan. I was scared. We had been on an amazing journey together for the previous 3 days, and I was scared that the next time we saw each other, it may be over for one, or even both of us. I shook his hand and said I expected to see him back at the camp soon. Duncan showed what I'd learned to be his customary class as a gent when he gave me a chuckle and said he'd be right behind me.

I checked I was good to go, and set off filled with a sense of drive and purpose. This wasn't like when Duncan suffered a nose bleed near the finish on Day 2 and told me to go ahead, when we both knew he could have crawled in and been ok, time wise. This was genuine 'is he going to be able to pull this out of the bag?' type worry. The Long Day of the MDS isn't to be taken lightly and I was petrified that it was going to ruin my new found friend's race. Equally, however, I was petrified it could be going to do the same to me. I was determined to put in a good show. As I saw it, if I was to limp along slowly, I may as well have stayed with Duncan. I had to make my selfish departure worth it. I had taken an mp3 player with me that had up until now gone unused. I felt this was as good a time as any to inject some motivation and distraction so pulled it out of my pocket and put my earphones in. The first song that came on was 'Go Your Own Way' by Fleetwood Mac. How apt! For the next couple of hours or so, I felt incredible. I was running whilst others around me were walking. Granted, some of this was because I had been overtaken by 'slower' competitors whilst sitting in the tent, but all the same, I was travelling at quite some speed. I could not believe how good I felt. We ran through a wide section to the course and I noticed, a long way to my right, my tent mate, Jorge. He was about 80 metres to my right, and looked in pain. I shouted to him, but he didn't hear me. I shouted once more, and when I got no response, tried to run across to him. I don't know what happened but I somehow lost sight of him. When I got over to where I thought he would be, he was nowhere to be seen. I can only assume that he had stopped when I wasn't looking and I had overshot him. I had a good look around but couldn't find him anywhere. It was a shame to have not been able to say 'hi,' but I reminded myself that this was all about me now and put my head back down. This was the self-affirming experience I had been searching for.

Around this time, I passed a major milestone; the first of today's two marathons. It had taken me around 10 hours, including our stops, which was good going given the lengthy stop at checkpoint 3. Mentally, getting the first marathon ticked off was a big deal. It meant that I was on the home leg. As I continued, I marveled at how good I was still feeling. Some of my high energy levels were to be expected given I had spent a fair old while resting at the previous checkpoint, but even so, I was pleasantly surprised. Bit by bit, the field started to thin out, and I had fewer competitors for 'company.' I had become very insular and wasn't looking to talk with any of them, but even so, the sight of other people was reassuring. It made me feel less vulnerable. As I continued though, I began to enjoy the solitude. It has always struck me as strange that people will pay good money to go into a gym and replicate what they could be doing outside in nature. There is something wonderfully pure about running. This was a favourite topic of conversation between me and my dad. The act of travelling over a pre-determined distance, on foot, as quick as possible is a brilliantly simple competition with both others, and oneself. And I was now in the most simple version of this most simple of sports. Me, against the desert. I was in my element and loving every second.

The terrain varied between hardstanding and loose sand. There were small clumps of shrubs dotted around the landscape, plus the all important route markers. A week or so before the event, a team goes out and marks the course. This is increasingly important on the long day when the field becomes more strung out, and it becomes harder for runners to simply follow the man in front. The markers are relatively simple; pink spray paint on anything suitable – rocks, trees, shrubs – anything appropriate. I continued ahead looking out for the markers and other runners, but both seemed in short supply. I was confident of my direction however, and kept up my pace. Half an hour of steady running later, and I thought my eyes were deceiving me. I could see what appeared to be a motorbike with 2 locals on the back, motoring towards me. I genuinely wondered if I was seeing things. This couldn't be possible however – I was in good shape, and not dehydrated. There was no way I could be hallucinating at this stage. I then began to worry; the bike was clearly heading straight towards me. It was about 100 metres away, but its direction of travel was clear. My worry heightened. One of the rules of the MDS is that you must keep your passport and €200 on you at all times. That wouldn't be bad loot for some local hijackers. The bike continued heading straight towards me. My heartrate started to go through the roof. The bike was about 50 metres away when I remember thinking, 'well this is disappointing. I came to the desert aware that I was putting myself in danger, but I thought it would be from dehydration, not a fucking mugging.' I was mentally preparing to dive out of the way of the bike when it got close to me, but was acutely aware that I didn't really have the energy to out run the bike, or the people on it for that matter!

And then it happened; the bike was on me like a flash. It got so close to me that I felt the air move. What happened? What did my would be assailants do? They shouted encouragement and rode off! They literally rode up to me, shouted 'Allez Monsieur, Allez Monsieur. Bonne chance!!.' After my initial bewilderment, I laughed my head off, and then felt a little embarrassed for the assumptions I had made. Even so, it was probably the most bizarre experience of my week. The course saw us now run across a dry river bed and then up a short steep incline through something vaguely resembling a hedge. At this point I saw a couple of fellow runners who were travelling quite slowly. I overtook them, taking care to give them both a slap on the back as I went past. 'Keep on going boys!'

I entered checkpoint 4 after 12 hours. By this point the light was starting to fade, and my energy levels were also starting to fade a touch. I walked into the checkpoint and sat myself down for a few minutes whilst taking on board an energy gel, some nuts and a good slug of water. When I came to stand back up though, my legs were incredibly stiff. They were the sort of stiff you encounter when you've just run a marathon, which was hardly surprising. The obvious issue I was facing was that I had just under another marathon left to go. I cursed myself repeatedly for allowing my legs to stiffen up, and vowed that I wouldn't stop again until the finish line. I noticed a stand offering the sweet tea that is normally at the finish line and hobbled over to take a cup. I was walking like I was wearing ski boots; mechanically, and clumsily. After drinking the tea I headed out of the camp but not before an official attached a glowstick to the rear of my backpack and reminded me that it was compulsory for all competitors to crack the stick and illuminate it once dusk has set in.

I headed out and gradually, step by step, my legs began to ease. It took approximately 30 minutes but eventually my legs returned to something approaching normal usage, all things considered. During this time, I spotted a few other runners; none of whom were using their headtorch. This surprised me as I was beginning to find it difficult to see. It took a good 10-15 minutes for me to realise that my problem was that I was still wearing my sunglasses... Maybe I was struggling mentally more than I realized. I took them off and enjoyed the last of the light before running alongside someone and asking them to crack my glowstick and fishing out my headtorch from my bumbag. I turned it on to a fairly low setting and continued on my way. I had overtaken the man who had helped me with my headtorch (after a quick 'Good luck buddy!' of course!) and was now on my own again. I put my headphones away and began to take in the enormity of my surrounds.

When dark, the Sahara is a remarkable place. It is so vast and open, and the sky so clear, that you almost feel joined to the starscape above you. The soft sand underfoot meant that my footsteps were making no noise whatsoever. The only sound was the rustling of my shorts as I marched, and my breathing. I felt as if I could be the only person on earth. My thoughts turned to my family. Lucy had been so incredibly supportive of this venture. I thought of her back home. She would likely be sat on the sofa having put the kids to bed. I wondered if this was what she imagined it would be like. I thought of Millie and Ted. Ted who was too young to understand what I was doing, and Millie who understood the broad principals but had blind faith in her dad who she believes can do anything. It was a truly magical moment as I marched ahead thinking of my family tucked up safe at home. I was thousands of miles away from them, in a starkly contrasted environment to them, but I had never felt so close to them. I knew how much both Lucy and Millie, and Ted in his own way, were willing me on, and it was a humbling feeling. I knew how proud they were of what I was trying to do. It gave me a boost of energy, and I reminded myself of one of the key reasons I was doing this. This was, in a large part, about proving to my children that they could achieve anything they wanted to, if they put the effort in, and believed in themselves. This was the most emotional I was to get during the entire week. I smiled to myself as I processed memories of my family whilst marching as fast as I could, and drinking in the view of the stars. I thought of just about every happy memory I could think of and drank in the details mentally. This was a welcome distraction, as well as being an extremely self-indulgent exercise that I rarely get a chance to enjoy in day to day life. I thought too, of my dad, but my thoughts and feelings quickly moved to my mum. My dad was a huge figure in my life, and I missed him dearly, but I couldn't help but think about my mum. She was still here, and living and breathing what I was doing. Mum is softer than dad who had an impressive resolve and set high standards. I knew mum would be proud of me no matter what I did out here on this dark, and increasingly chilly evening. I also knew however, that she would be almost feeling my experience twice. Once for her, and a second time for my dad. I knew that *she knew* how happy dad would be if I could get the job done.

I think I must have lost over an hour in my daydreams and before long I realised that the next checkpoint would be coming up. By this point I had two fresh problems. The first was relatively minor in the grand scheme of things, but irritating all the same – my watch was running low on battery. Whilst not essential, I really didn't want to have to travel 'blind' as to my distance. I decided that if needs be, I would use the GPS function on my phone to guide me in. The second was far more serious. My left foot was starting to give me an acute pain just back from my toes. It only happened every now and then, which made me suspect that I had a tiny stone in my shoe. Knowing the checkpoint was not far off, I thought I would wait until I could investigate things more easily under the lighting, so pushed ahead. I didn't see anyone else until I got to checkpoint 5, which represented 56.1km done, in 14hr2m.

Checkpoint 5 had been designated as one of the 'sleep stations.' There were a few people in tents already trying to grab some sleep, as well as a group of people doing their best to stop them from sleeping, by singing around a camp fire! I remembered my vow to not stop until the finish and took my water, took an energy gel and ate a Grenade bar before going straight through the mini-camp and out of the exit to continue onto the course. In doing so, I don't know how, but I completely forgot to investigate my problem with my left foot. I can only assume that I was so focused on the job in hand, and in *not* stopping, that it completely slipped my mind.

As I left the checkpoint, I did a few calculations in my head. At the rate I was going, I thought I would finish in something between 18h30m and 19h30m. it was difficult to be certain because my pace was definitely slowing. This would mean running until around 3am. By this point, it was around 11pm, and starting to get quite cold. I tried to force myself to keep the pace up. I had approximately 18 miles left to go, which was still a heck of a long way, and I was now officially into the territory of running the furthest I had ever run. I took pride in the fact that every step was a new personal distance record. Around this time, however, my physical condition started to deteriorate and deteriorate fast, whilst my frame of mind also took a turn for the worse. I was hitting the wall. I could feel it happening as each step became increasingly tough. I kept looking at my watch as it was imperative I was up to date on the total distance travelled for when my battery failed. I could then start up my phone and add the two distances together to gauge how far to the next checkpoint, and ultimately, the finish line.

I looked at my watch; 16 miles to go. (I realise I keep switching between kms and miles, but they measure the course in kms and I mentally always calculate in miles!) I started to break things down into more achievable goals. If I could grit my teeth for 3 miles, which is basically a Park Run, then there would only be a half marathon left. Then, if I could grit my teeth for another 3 miles, I would be down to single figures, miles wise. Another 4 miles of pain, and it would only be a 10km. Then a 5km, and then just a mile to the finish. I was in a dark place mentally, but this approach was my best bet of getting the job done. The harsh reality is I was in agony. Hitting the wall, running, is a horrendous experience. With every step you take, your body tells you to stop. I'd hit the wall once at the London Marathon, following no training, with 13 miles left. Here, I was going to have to travel a full 3 miles further than that, having already run 3 times the distance. This was going to be everything I hoped it would be, whilst also being everything I *feared* it would be.

I began talking to myself. 'No-one's going to do this for you. Just grit your teeth, accept that pain is just another sensation that WILL pass, and get it done. Just get it fucking done. No excuses, no being a baby. Just get the fucking thing done.' I started repeating a phrase in my head, over and over and over. 'One step, two step, keep moving forward. One step, two step, keep moving forward.' Time was passing so slowly. I couldn't believe how slowly I was travelling. Each mile was taking me 20 minutes by this point. Crucially though, I was still moving forward. As long as I could keep moving in a forward direction, I knew I would get there in the end. I knew I'd be ok. '*One step, two step, keep moving forward...*'

By this point, I was not quite zombie-like, but certainly not of particularly coherent thought. It became a very basic existence. Keep one foot moving in front of the other and don't get lost. I didn't need to worry about drinking heaps of water because it had turned relatively cold and my sweat rate had dropped. It was important though, that I kept drinking my electrolyte solution, so I focused on that. As I moved, I 'zoned out.' At 40 years old, this was probably the most free I'd felt in the 20 or so years since I'd been a student. Literally, nothing else mattered other than getting myself to the finish line. In a world of young children, mortgages, client deadlines and the general treadmill of life, this was a truly amazing experience. It had been like it all week, to be honest, but right now, in the pitch black, running on my own, pitting myself against the desert, the sensation was lifted to new heights.

Moving along, all of a sudden, my head torch flashed. Or didn't it flash? I couldn't be sure... But if it *did* flash, was that a sign that the batteries were low? I didn't think there was any chance they could be low as they had been brand new before I had turned them on just a short time before. But what if they were duff batteries?! I started to worry, but reminded myself that I had spare batteries in my backpack for exactly this eventuality. Even if they were faulty batteries, and they did run out quicker than expected, I had some spares that I had intentionally taken from a different packet that I had bought from a different shop, in case one pack had been from a faulty batch. I'd be ok, so there was no need to worry. It was just one more example of the requirement for mind-over-matter.

My watch beeped and finally died when I had 15 miles left. I pulled my phone out of the sidepocket on my backpack and fired up the Strava app. At this point I realised that I was behaving like I was drunk. My co-ordination was poor and I was clumsy. I remembered a time I had been forced, with 2 mates, to walk 10 or so miles in the middle of the night, following the end of a house party, and a taxi-no-show. We'd all been pretty drunk when doing that, and I now chuckled at the accidental training it had provided me with. 15 miles to go. *'One step, two step, keep moving forward.'*

Getting to checkpoint 6 was a major target. Once I had hit checkpoint 6, it was only 10km to the seventh and final checkpoint, and then only another 9km to the finish. There was no getting away from the fact that I was struggling physically, and also in a lot of pain, and moving very slowly, but I was still moving. Around this time, the terrain turned to firm sand dunes that presented themselves like very pronounced ridge & furrow fields. What this meant was that for half the time, I couldn't see the course markers, because I was in the valley of the furrow. I'd shuffle (marching had stopped a long way back) up onto the brow of the dune, and scan for the next marker, before descending down into the furrow where I wouldn't be able to see anything beyond the sand immediately in front of me. My fear now was going off course. I wasn't too bothered about getting lost per sae, however I was extremely keen to not end up running additional, unnecessary miles. Every now and then I would see a marker in the distance that looked like it was moving – other runners! I stumbled on.

Seeing checkpoint 6 in the background was in a strange way, both positive and negative. It was positive because I was getting closer to the finish line, but also negative because it took me out of my daze for long enough to realise that I was going to once again be a long way from my next target, of checkpoint 7. I entered the checkpoint rather like a drunk trying to blag their way into a nightclub. The key difference here, was that the people I was trying to converse with were sympathetic and helpful, rather than surly bouncers! I said 'checkpoint six, oui?' They confirmed this and said 'just 21 kilometres to go, Duncan. YOU CAN DO IT!!.' I stopped to fill up my bottles and then instantly carried on walking. I knew my energy levels were low, but thought I stood a better chance of getting the day finished if I forced myself to keep going. Should I stop to rest, I knew that I wouldn't get up again for a few hours. Whilst this wouldn't have been the end of the world in terms of completing the day within the allowed time, it would be a failure in my own mind, given the goal I had set myself before the event, and then the day itself.

There was 11km between checkpoint 6 and checkpoint 7, so I broke it down into 2x 4km sections, and then a 3km section. I put all of my emotional and mental energy into imagining a force behind my back forcing me to keep going; pushing me on. I told myself that no matter how bad I was feeling, I could keep on going.

A few years previously, I had read about an experiment where a scientist had requested some reasonably fit people cycle on static bikes until they were *so exhausted that they could not continue. They cycled until they were absolutely shattered at which point they gave up. The scientist offered them $1,000 if they could cycle flat out for a further 60 seconds. They all managed the additional 60 seconds. He then offered them $2,000 if they could manage a further 30 seconds. Again, they all managed it. I can't remember how long exactly the experiment went on for, but the finding was clear – your mind gives up before your body.*

I kept telling myself that no matter how bad I was feeling, if I stopped, I was choosing to give up. The important word here was 'choosing.' I wasn't prepared to do this, and fortunately, was able to balance off the long-term satisfaction I knew I would feel when I finished, versus the short-term agony I was in at the time. It was at this point, however, that my left foot flared up again, and did so quite spectacularly. Having not caused me any discomfort for an hour or so, my left foot felt like I was treading on a drawing pin. I then realised that both feet were extremely sore on my heels as well. I quickly came to the conclusion that this was par for the course given what I was trying to do, and that I would do my best to ignore it. I would have virtually a whole day to recuperate if I could get finished before daybreak.

By this point, my stride length had shortened considerably, and my leg speed was verging on a slow limp. I felt absolutely terrible. This was probably the worst I had felt in my entire life. It was like waking up with a terrible bout of flu, the sorest feet you've ever had, and sporadic nausea, and then being told to walk 20km+ through a pitch-black desert. As much as I was struggling though, in a sadomasochistic way, I was sort of enjoying it. I knew that I wasn't in any danger, but that I was pushing my body to its absolute limit. That, in itself, is a fantastic feeling. In a modern world designed to make life as easy and comfortable as possible, pushing your body and mind to their very, very limits is a remarkable sensation.

Given how I was feeling, I knew that if I was able to keep going and finish the stage without having to rest, the achievement would be something that I could draw on in my wider life for years to come. I remembered my realisation that I find it easier to make myself do something I don't want to, than not do something I do want to. I did want to finish, and I *didn't* want to stop. Was that the right way round, or the wrong way round? I couldn't work it out! Either way, this was all down to will power.

I exited the checkpoint with no-one ahead of me to tag onto, and seemingly no-one keen to follow up behind. I was on my own. My headtorch hadn't flashed again, so I assumed I'd probably imagined it. I shuffled on, deliberately trying to disengage my brain. It was a bit like when you wake up in the night because you need the loo, and try to get out of bed, go to the loo, and get back into bed; all without properly waking up. This was my own attempt at an induced coma. A matter of 30-40 minutes ago, I was enjoying myself despite the pain. Now though, I was reveling in the challenge, but hating every second of the battle. I looked at my phone; 10km to checkpoint 7. I'd shuffled the previous kilometre in 12 minutes. My 10km best was 33 minutes, a very long time ago. I wouldn't manage 3km in that time. Through my daze, I remembered my dear old dad saying to me once when I was training for a marathon, 'the thing is, whilst running quicker is going to tire you out son, it also means you get the job done sooner!' It's a very obvious point, but also a valid one. Treat the distance like ripping off a plaster. I tried to force myself into a run but only lasted about 10 metres before I gave up.

Nothing newsworthy happened for the next hour, other than the fact that my foot was absolute agony, and I shuffled in complete isolation. I literally did not see another soul; nor did I hear anything other than the sound of my own footsteps and breathing. It was surreal. Then I heard faint voices behind me. It sounded like a few people together, and female voices. The thought of some company lifted my spirits and I hoped they would catch me up, however I wasn't willing to slow down in order to facilitate this. I was still desperate to get this finished as soon as possible. 10 minutes later, they caught me up. I looked at my phone; 9km to the next checkpoint. I was travelling at a consistent 5km an hour. By this point, my foot was causing me incredible pain, but I didn't want to risk taking any codeine. It was dark and I was typically travelling on my own. If I suffered any side-effects, I could end up in a very precarious situation.

'Hello Duncan, how are you my good man?!' came the extremely cheerful, and jolly posh greeting from one of the ladies. It instantly snapped me out of my self-pity. 'I'm good thanks, how are you guys?' I attempted to chirp. 'Well, I don't know about you my good man Duncan, but I'm totally fucking bollocksed to be fair. And if you're telling me you're good, I have a sneaking suspicion you may be telling me lies, you scoundrel, you.' I chuckled. 'Yeah, I'm in bits to be honest.' 'Don't take any notice of her; she always gets like this when she's over-tired!' said one of the other girls. They were just what I needed at that moment in time. Fun, bubbling with energy, and forcing me to talk with them. We walked together and chatted about life back home.

After 30 minutes or so though, my foot felt too painful to continue. I told them I needed to stop. They asked me if I'd like them to stop with me to help which was an incredibly kind gesture. I told them I would be fine, and they continued. I stopped, and sat down. On sitting down, I quickly realised I had a problem. I couldn't actually bend my leg enough to be able to undo my shoe. The moment I got close, it felt like I was going to get serious cramp, which history told me, I would be unable to shake off. I sat, weighing up my options. If I tried to get my shoe off, I could end up with significant cramp. I may then end up unable to put it back on again. I'd have to just carry on regardless. I went to get up, and found that having sat down, I couldn't get back up onto my feet. After 20 or 30 seconds of rolling around like a turtle on its back, I looked up to see where the group of ladies had got to and whether they could help me. I shouted out, but they had disappeared over the brow of a hill.

This moment, right here, was both my lowest point during the week, and also my highlight when I look back on the event. The 30 seconds that followed are what all of the dreaming and training had been about. This was when I was going to find out a few things about myself. I lay on my back, looking up into the sky, completely alone. I had nothing left; yet knew I needed to find more. This wasn't me versus the other competitors. Nor was it me versus the desert. This was me versus me. I suddenly roared at the top of my voice until my lungs emptied. It was a visceral, almost primeval noise that I made without any forethought. I'm still not sure what prompted me to do it. I remember screaming and gritting my teeth. I rolled onto my side, pulled my legs up into the foetal position with my arms, and then rolled onto my front. I was now in a position where I could push myself up with my arms and gradually put my feet under myself.

Once upright, I had to get my legs moving again. If I had thought they were stiff at checkpoint 4, this was a whole new level. I was walking like C3PO out of Star Wars. But I had done it; I'd got myself moving again. I set myself a target of catching up with the ladies I'd previously been with. This was good as it meant my goal was something smaller and more attainable than 'get to the checkpoint.' I put my headphones in and 'Let it Go,' from the kids' film, Frozen came on. This instantly made me smile. I have lost count of the amount of times I've danced round the kitchen and sung this at the top of my voice with my daughter. Like most 6 year olds, Millie absolutely loves it, and I love joining in her enjoyment of it. So at that precise moment, the Sahara Desert (or at least the area immediately surrounding me) was filled with the sound of a 40 year old man from Warwickshire singing *Let it Go* as loud as is humanly possible. It was incredible! It made me feel close to my daughter and both cheered and invigorated me no end.

As I write, I realise that it must come across like my energy levels and emotions were all over the place; trying to zone out one minute, roaring, shouting, singing at the top of my voice the next. That is the reality of what was happening. It was a complete rollercoaster. Up one minute, down the next. But the pain was a constant. Both my left foot specifically, and everywhere else beyond that, as a dull deep-seated sense of total emptiness throbbing. I crested a small hill and looked down ahead of me. I could see some lights bobbing, and was fairly confident it would be the ladies I'd just been with. They were about 300m ahead of me so I put some effort into catching them. 15 minutes later and I was back with them. 'Hello ladies, you can't get rid of me that easily... fancy towing me into the checkpoint please?' 'Duncan you lazy bastard, we thought you'd stopped for a sleep! Of course! But don't go behind her, she keeps farting.' There was a little under 5km to the checkpoint, and we all trudged on together but in silence by this point. An hour until the checkpoint... an hour until the home stretch. It was no longer about speed, or finishing times, but all about just finishing at all.

Following an hour of wincing each time I put my left foot down, I saw the checkpoint in the distance. A few minutes later and we all entered the checkpoint together. One of the ladies asked me if I would like help to look at my foot but I politely declined. I thought I could put up with the pain, and didn't want to slow them up. They sat down and tended to various issues, whilst I ate a cliff bar. Just as they started to shape to get back on the road, I suddenly decided I should look at my foot. I didn't feel I could ask them for help, so sat down to do it myself. It was incredibly difficult. I pawed at my gaiter trying to free up my laces; all the time worrying that I would get cramp. It took about 5 minutes but I eventually managed to take my shoe off and start to prepare some tape and padding to go under the painful area. One of the Doc Trotters came over and asked if I am ok. I tried to convince her to help me with the strapping but she was firm in her refusal. It took me a further 5 minutes to arrange the strapping in a vaguely effective fashion. I put my shoe back on, only to realise I hadn't put my gaiter on first, so had to repeat the process. It wasn't so much the time factor that bothered me, but more that my brain was functioning so badly that it was extremely hard work. The official came back over to talk to me, and just as I sorted my shoe, I began to shake violently. The shaking was so severe it must have looked like I was having a fit. The lady said something about 'hypothermia' and that she was going to get a doctor. I wasn't concerned though, and definitely didn't want a doctor getting involved. I had just got a bit cold, and had low blood sugar. I grabbed my down jacket out of my bag, put it on and clambered to my feet. Whether it was easier to stand up because my legs had improved, or because I was panicked about an interfering doctor, I'll never know, but I certainly got to my feet quicker than I had done previously. I fished out some sweets from my pack, put my pack on my back and set off again, munching as I went.

I continued to shake for only 2-3 minutes, before returning to my normal state of feeling absolutely terrible. This was it; this was the home stretch. And now I was back moving again, I knew I would be ok. I knew I would get it done. This wasn't premature or misplaced confidence; just a realisation that I knew myself well enough to know that I wasn't going to give up on an 86km race after completing 76km!

I'd hoped to catch the 3 ladies up, but they were long gone. Probably 1km ahead of me. (They would ultimately finish 14 minutes ahead of me). I was back to being on my own. This felt appropriate to me. The long day had always been a very personal challenge, so completing it on my own felt somehow fitting. I suddenly thought of Duncan and realised I hadn't given him a single thought for the previous 6 or 7 hours. I felt pretty grotty about that, but thought it was understandable all things considered. I wondered how he was getting on. Had he managed to continue? I so very much hoped so.

The following 90 minutes were the longest of my life, with absolutely no exaggeration, and also extremely emotional. I wasn't crying, but I was on the edge, emotionally. The problem I now faced was that the 'lump in my throat' was making it more difficult to breathe. It was incredible how slow time could pass – and more importantly, how slow I was moving. My phone confirmed that I was making progress – just very, very slowly. I quietly repeated the lyrics to 'Dream On' by Aerosmith. They were so relevant.

> Every time when I look in the mirror
> All these lines on my face getting clearer
> The past is gone
> It went by, like dusk to dawn
> Isn't that the way
> Everybody's got the dues in life to pay
>
> I know nobody knows
> Where it comes and where it goes
> I know it's everybody sin
> You got to lose to know how to win
>
> Half my life
> Is books, written pages
> Live and learn from fools and
> From sages
> You know it's true, oh
> All these feelings come back to you
>
> Dream on
> Dream on
> Dream on
> Dream until your dreams come true

I was determined that this lifelong dream was going to come true. I was also aware that it was all within my control. It was just a case of how much I wanted it. Everyone thinks they want things. But do they want them enough? If this dream was a hot coal in a fire, was I prepared to endure the pain it would take to pull it out and claim it?

Lucy once said that I have a switch in my head that I flick when things get tough. She's always laughed at the state I would finish up in at the end of some training sessions. I'd be sweating, puking and prostrate on the floor, and Lucy would say 'why do you do this to yourself? *How* do you do this to yourself?' I'd typically lie there chuckling and thinking, 'why would you not?!' She's right in one way in that I can make a mental decision that the rational side of my brain needs to overpower the emotional side, but I also firmly believe that everyone has this switch. It just sometimes takes a while to find it.

Back in the desert, I went into zombie mode. '*One step, two step, keep moving forward. One step, two step, keep moving forward.*' I saw a few headtorches in the distance and tried to run. It was no good, I had nothing left. I pushed on, again imagining a force behind me pushing me forward.

I watched an interview with Muhammad Ali once where he described his third fight with Joe Frazier. He said something along the lines of 'the places I had to go to mentally, in order to beat that man, are places I never want to have to go to again.' As exhausting as the MDS was, I wouldn't disrespect boxing (particularly not legendary all-time greats such as these!) by comparing the two, however I was about to enter my own version of this particular sensation. Whilst knowing I would be 'ok,' I also knew the best way I'd get it done was by flicking the switch Lucy refers to, harnessing all of the emotions I'd ever felt in my life, both good and bad, and using them as a fuel. I thought about all of my disappointments over the years; in sport, in work, in my personal life. I thought about teachers who had told me I would never amount to anything if I didn't take life more seriously. I thought about my granddad. I thought about my dad, and how much he would have loved this (whilst also thinking it was highly irresponsible!). I thought about how his death cheated me out of enjoying my kids with him. I then thought about asking Lucy to marry me and her saying yes, and the birth of our two children. I thought about my emails from Millie telling me 'she just knew I could do it.' I thought about all of my friends back home who were willing me on. I thought about the hours of training, and associated hours of time away from my family. I balled it all up inside myself like a fire, and used it to drive myself forward.

And then I saw the inflatable finish line. It looked about 2km away. Renewed with energy, I tried to break into a jog, but reverted to a walk within 20 or 30 seconds. I pushed on though, still wincing with every pace. As I got closer, I heard voices behind me. By this stage, I was approximately 1km from the finish line and I really didn't want to be caught on the way in. I thought of Lucy at home, potentially watching me finish despite the anti-social time. I didn't want her to see me struggling, or being 'caught on the line.' I attempted a jog again. This time however, I managed to keep it going! *(Back to the fact that you are rarely ever truly physically exhausted...)* I attempted to speed up, and looked down at my phone. I was running at 8min mile pace. This was ludicrous! For the previous 4 or 5 hours I had been unable to travel at anything quicker than 20 minute mile pace and now I was more than double that speed! I was determined, though, that the voices behind would not catch me. The lights of the finish line were approaching now, and as I drew nearer I realised that I was overtaking some other competitors who had been running a slightly different line on the course to me. I ran past them and shouted encouragement. 2 minutes later, I crossed the line in 18h55min.

I had long wondered what my emotional state would be, if I did ever manage to complete the long day of the MDS. I wondered if I would shout from the rooftops, or attempt a cartwheel, or just quietly sob into my recovery drink. The reality was, as I crossed the line and exchanged pleasantries with the official, I didn't know how to feel. I just felt totally wrung out. It was as if I had insufficient emotional energy to cheer or to cry. But standing there, accepting my sweet tea,

I gave myself a small smile. I HAD DONE IT. It may sound strange, but I clearly remember my relief at feeling the metaphorical bundling up and putting to one side the emotional force I had been using to force myself forward. It was a serene moment as I looked up into the dark sky, and gave my fist the smallest of clenches.

As soon as I stopped and tried to gather stock, I realised I was in trouble. My legs started to turn, not quite to jelly, but certainly out of my own control. As I tried to pick up and carry my water, I staggered a few paces and one official ordered another to come to my assistance. An elderly gentleman came over and asked me what tent I was in. He was kind and reassuring and offered to carry my water for me. Even at this stage though, I had an ingrained belief that allowing someone else to carry my water, even within the bivouac to our tent, was tantamount to cheating. I did, however, gratefully follow his direction.

On arriving at my tent, I said 'thank you' and set about trying to sort myself out. I saw 3 bodies in sleeping bags in the tent and tried to have a peek to see who they were. I had a fair idea who it would probably be, and was right. Paul, Mark & Dee were back. This was great news; with my arrival, we were half way to a full tent! As I looked into the tent, Dee's head popped up like a meercat. Dee is one of the most happy, smiley, cheerful people I've ever met and it was a delight to be met by her beaming personality. She asked me how I was doing and if I needed any help. I tried to engage but, as wonderful as it was to see her, I was totally washed out. She asked me where Duncan was. I told her what had happened as I pulled my sleeping bag out, and also mentioned I'd seen Jorge. I then mixed up a recovery shake and started to try to force it down. Literally, each gulp made me wretch. I thought I was going to puke over my sleeping bag at one point, but I knew how vital it was that I got it inside me within a short space of finishing.

I pulled my shoes off, climbed into my sleeping bag, pulled the hood over my head, and lay back. As soon as I did, I got the most intense cramp I'd ever felt; in a place that I'd never experienced cramp before. It was a muscle somewhere deep in my groin, between my legs, and below my arse cheeks. The problem I had was that I didn't know how to 'stretch it out,' and even if I did, I was pretty much in the leg equivalent of a straight-jacket, given the dimensions of my sleeping bag. I spent a few minutes rotating and 'pointing' my feet to see if I could relieve things. I was in incredibly intense pain. I turned to Dee, 'what's the cut off time for the next marathon stage, Dee?' She didn't answer me directly. 'Don't worry Nellie; you're going to be fine,' she responded. It was the most simple, caring answer, possible at that moment in time, and one more example of how close to and in tune with your tent mates you become. Eventually, the cramp subsided a touch and I must have fallen to sleep at around 4am.

I woke and looked at my watch. It was 5:30am. I sat up and looked over at Dee, who was still beaming. She and I spent a few minutes quietly discussing our experiences, before I lay back down again. The great news was that the majority of the pain in my legs had subsided. Listening, the atmosphere in the bivouac was strange; a lot of people were lying asleep, a lot of people were sat up wearily chatting, whilst other people were returning in dribs and drabs. It was very fragmented. I decided I wasn't remotely ready for the day to start so put my head back down. Before I did, however, I noticed another body in our tent. I shuffled over to see who it was. Jorge! Get in! We were now five eighths complete! He was fast asleep and looked totally broken. I gently tapped his arm. *Good work, Jorge; you the man.*

I next woke a couple of hours later and there was significantly more movement within the bivouac. I sat up; properly this time. In the tent were Paul, Mark, Dee, Jorge and me. Jorge was still dead to the world. The rest of us all began to share our stories with each other. I can't remember a lot about the discussion. No matter the detail of what was being discussed, my thoughts kept returning to Duncan. Was he making good progress? How would we find out if he had stopped? Half an hour or so later, I cooked myself some breakfast –

although breakfast today was beef stroganoff. It was amazing! It felt like when you wake up after a heavy night out, and eat left over pizza – it was one of the best meals I had ever had! I finished it and lay back down. Unbelievably, my legs didn't actually feel too bad, and despite the agony whilst running, my feet weren't causing me untoward pain.

We all lay there for an hour or so, and then I heard footsteps approaching our tent. I heard Mark cheer 'heeeeyyyyy!' and I looked up. It was Duncan! Walking in, as cool, calm and collected as I should have expected. I felt like crying. 'Dunc! You made it big man!' I exclaimed. 'Of course, buddy. Never in doubt was it?' he smiled with typical understatement. I cannot explain how happy seeing Duncan made me.

Duncan explained that he had waited for a couple of hours when I'd left him and then grabbed a small amount of sleep at one of the checkpoints. I was in awe of what he had done. To force himself to start again after such a lengthy rest, and then again after a sleep, struck me as being incredible. He lay down for a rest and we all did our best to be quiet to not disturb him or the (still snoring) Jorge. With only Charlotte and Jules still out there, I became certain of two things:

1) We were going to have a full complement in our tent after the long stage
2) We were going to have a full complement in our tent at the conclusion of the entire race

There was no way Charlotte and Jules weren't going to finish the long stage. Those two were made of granite. They may not have been the quickest in the tent, but they were definitely the most resolute. Jules always had this unflappable air about him when it came to his running. He seemed to have encountered most things and knew what to do to overcome the challenges that would be thrown up. Charlotte was quieter but had a kind of understated determination in her eyes that I'd seldom seen before. It seemed to me that Charlotte may well have been the hardest person I'd ever met. It was just a matter of when those guys joined us in the tent.

And given I was confident that we would all complete the long stage, I was just as confident that we would all complete the race in its entirety. The next day was just a regular marathon, and then we'd have the medal around our neck. That I've written 'just a regular marathon' demonstrates how the MDS stretches what you believe you're capable of. Sitting there, I began to look forward to the final marathon stage. I thought it would be fun to go all out, without holding anything back for any subsequent stages. How misplaced my confidence was to turn out to be!

A couple of hours later, sure enough, Jules and Charlotte appeared. YEEESSSSSS!!! Tent 143 was complete. We all welcomed them into the tent and listened to their adventure. One of the things that I loved about the MDS is that you all run the same course, but all have completely different adventures. Your individual experience is dictated by the time of day you hit each part of the course, how many people you are with, and the specific people you interact with throughout the day. Plus, of course, your personal perspective. A steep incline that I may have found extraordinarily tough because I hit it in the heat of the day, with a traffic jam of runners queuing to use a guidance rope, may have been a lot easier for someone quicker or slower than me who had gone through when it was cooler and less busy. Similarly, one person my hate every step of the incline on a jebel due to the associated pain, whereas the next person loves it due to their excitement at the view they would encounter at the top. I found it fascinating and enthralling listening to how other people had gone.

The remainder of the day was a mixture of rest and recuperation. I was concerned about my left foot and took a trip to Doc Trotters. They weren't a great deal of help, but I'm not sure there was a lot they could do. There was no overt damage to the area that was causing me most pain. I became a little concerned that I may have suffered a stress-fracture, but put it to the back of my mind. There was nothing I could do about it if I had; it was best to just not think about it. The medical team gave me some gauze that I folded up to make into padding, with a view to cushioning the offending area. We milled around the bivouac and went and chatted with other runners. There was a lovely atmosphere that day. I've tried hard to find a better word than 'lovely' but it best sums the day up. All you could hear was soft, weary talking and laughing. The sense of 'a job well done.' No matter how the day had gone, the vast majority of people were grateful to have finished. 25 competitors were forced to pull out during the long stage, which whilst devastating for them individually, I didn't think was too bad overall.

We strolled round to keep our legs moving. I took a trip to the email tent and sent a message home. I thought the email provision was an incredible service offered by the organisers. It struck me as really going above and beyond. I don't think one could have moaned if they took the attitude that 'you're in the desert, incommunicado for a week.' Later, I had a chat with Duncan about how he was feeling. I initially felt bad for him. He was such a strong athlete; much stronger than me. It was a real shame that he'd hit difficulties and it didn't seem fair. But talking to him, I realised that he didn't feel bad for himself. Duncan was taking it in his stride and viewing it as all part of the rich tapestry that makes up the MDS. He'd enjoyed his own adventure just as much as I'd enjoyed mine. I scolded myself for patronising him with pity.

The MDS is such an individual thing, and for the overwhelming majority, the goal is just to finish. Sure, there are the elite runners who are looking for placings, and I guess even the mid-packers like me had a quarter of an eye on trying to move up the leader board each day, if at all possible. Overall however, this pales into insignificance versus your own battle with self. You can't allow other people's lives and achievements to impact on your own sense of worth and happiness. Figuratively speaking, your neighbour's £10, doesn't make your £5 worth any less. You go on a holiday you love, and your friend goes on a 'better' holiday. Does that affect your enjoyment of your own holiday? Of course not. Or at least it shouldn't. To allow it to is effectively handing the key to your happiness to someone else. You can only control your life and your happiness should be founded in what you can control. The MDS is the perfect embodiment of this philosophy. Everyone seemed happy in themselves, and happy for everyone else. In my eyes, my placing within the race was worth no more and no less than anyone else's.

As we walked, I turned to Duncan and asked him, 'run together tomorrow mate?' 'It'd be a pleasure buddy,' he responded. What a gent. We decided we'd give it a bit of stick on the marathon stage. Or at least empty the tank fully, and leave nothing out on the course.

A few things stand out from the remainder of the 'rest' day. Firstly, the organisers gave each competitor a can of ice-cold Coca-Cola. Following close on a week of drinking nothing but tepid water through a rubber valve, this was eutopia. I actually collected my can and took it back to the tent, delaying opening it. I wanted to set aside some time to savour it. Whenever I have finished a long run, my body craves two things; mature cheddar cheese and full fat coke. I don't know why, but it happens every time. To have one of these offered up was a real treat! As I sat in the tent sipping my can, so as to savour the sugar rush for as long as possible I suddenly realised that I hadn't seen my sunglasses in ages. I'd been enjoying walking around the bivouac with no socks, no gaiters and no sunglasses. But where the hell were they? I thought back to where I had put them when I'd quickly taken them off the previous evening, on realising I was the only one stupid enough to still be wearing them! I didn't remember putting them in my bag. I think I had just tucked them into the loop of my bumbag. If that *was* the case, I'd lost them. I rifled through all of the relevant places but couldn't find them. This was far from ideal. How was I going to run a full marathon through a desert with no shades to protect my eyes from the sand, and just as importantly, the sun?

I thought there must have been a lost property box at the main desk in the camp. I walked over and as I did thought to myself, 'what am I going to do if they have some glasses, but they're not mine?' I wrestled with this for all of approximately 2 seconds. I'd take them. I spoke with a man at the desk and explained my situation. He said 'no problem; look in that box. Take anything you can use.' Fortunately, my worry over taking someone else's glasses was short-lived. This wasn't a lost property box as such, but more a collection of random shit. Some of it seemed to bare no relevance to the task of crossing a desert. (An umbrella, or a pillow anyone?). There were a couple of pairs of glasses and I picked one pair out. 'What were the chances?!' I said in mock surprise to the man behind the desk. He laughed and said in a strong French accent, 'It must be your lucky day, go on, take them!' As I returned to the camp I still felt a degree of embarrassment that these weren't my glasses so tried to avoid too much conversation about them!

Walking around the camp that evening was something to behold. Some of the sights were incredible. Whilst most people were in reasonable shape, there was also a heck of a lot of people who were in a mess. Seemingly every direction I looked in offered up someone limping along with the shortest of strides. I walked past the Doc Trotter tent and stuck my head in out of nosiness. I was met by a long line of people sat cleaning their feet. All of them were wincing with pain and some of them were crying. Their feet were in appalling condition, with open wounds, burst blisters and blood oozing from sores. Despite their evident pain however, everyone seemed quietly resolute. They knew they would get themselves sorted and in shape to continue the following day. The trashed feet were a danger that we all had known was a possibility. Whilst my feet were painful, I thanked my blessings that I was not anywhere close to being in the state of my comrades stretched out in front of me.

An hour or so later, and the bivouac began to buzz. The word was that the last runner was approaching the finish line. We all flocked to the finish in anticipation. It took a while to pick him out, but before too long we spotted a figure bent double, limping toward the finish. The figure was roughly 200m away. As it approached; painfully slowly, I thought my eyes were deceiving me. The man appeared to be in his 70s, and literally bent double – but sideways. This was incredible. The strength of mind, and body, was astonishing. As he approached, the entire bivouac flooded around him cheering whilst clearing a path for him to walk. Patrick Bauer walked at his side, as did Rachid El Morabity who was the race leader.

There were an awful lot of faces with tears running down them. Slowly but surely, he made it to the finish line. It was an incredible moment when he crossed the line. I've watched a lot of sport. As a lifelong rugby fan, I've watched the British Lions face the All Blacks in New Zealand. I've watched Usain Bolt, Jessica Ennis-Hill, Haile Gebrselassie and Allyson Felix run live in person. And just about every major sporting event from the Ryder Cup to the World Snooker, I've watched on TV, live. This however, is probably my favourite sporting 'moment.' It had taken him 34h08m39s. He finished over an hour slower than the next nearest competitor. But he had finished and the sense of collective enjoyment amongst all those who witnessed it was palpable. Try telling anyone who witnessed this spectacle that this warrior, who was aged 72, had achieved less in finishing last, than Rachid El Morabity had in finishing first. This was what it was all about. If ever there was an embodiment of everyone supporting each other, and willing each other on, this was it. I found the moment quite overwhelming. This man represented everything that I felt the MDS, and running in general in fact, is all about. You're not battling with the other runners, but with the little voice in your head telling you to stop. I couldn't imagine how much this guy must have wanted to stop throughout the previous double-marathon he had just completed. Yet he had kept going, and made it to the finish line. I was in awe.

Afterwards, we walked back to our tent, all in amazement at what we had just seen. If we needed one, which we most definitely didn't, it was the perfect motivation for the day to come. That night, we all went through our packs and threw out anything other than mandatory items and the bare minimum nutrition for the next day and breakfast on the charity day. With just the marathon left to go, everyone wanted their pack to be as light as possible. Jules had developed a bit of a reputation for having all sorts in his pack. Most days he would say 'does anyone want a spare ....' The offering would be anything from some strapping, to toilet paper, to batteries, to headphones. It was incredible that his pack didn't weigh three times ours! That night he said 'I've got a spare Tailwind here. Does anyone want it?' I'd used more of my electrolyte tablets than I'd intended and was running low, so said I'd gladly take it. And this decision right here, was about to cause me major problems.

Tailwind is a well-known brand of endurance fuel. Jules had the sachets of powder that you dissolve in your water. I had never drunk the stuff before, yet somehow was stupid enough to not consider this before putting it on top of my bag for the morning.

Jules also offered me an Oxo cube to make a hot drink with. It was incredible what Jules could offer up from his pack. It became something of a joke in our tent. Each night, he would rustle through his pack and say 'anyone fancy a energy gel?' Or 'anyone make use of some spare strapping?' Or 'anyone need any spare batteries?' If he'd said 'anyone need a spare cam belt for a 1983 Ford Capri?' it really wouldn't have surprised me! How his pack didn't weigh 50kg, I'll never understand. His offer of an Oxo cube was gratefully received however, and it tasted absolutely fantastic.

We went to sleep that night, all happy and content. We were within touching distance of our goal.

CHAPTER 16

Day 6 – 42.2km

woke up feeling on top of the world. Just a marathon to go, and I'd have achieved the goal I'd been chasing for quite literally, half my life. The mood in the camp was upbeat. Everyone was marveling at how light their pack felt. I was eager to get going. My legs, surprisingly, felt ok. My left foot was a problem, but I could grin and bear that for the sake of getting the job done. I emptied the Tailwind into one of my bottles, and filled the other with pure water.

I had packed myself a spare pair of socks for use the day after the long day. I'd read on one of the blogs that this was a great thing to do as it made your feet feel very refreshed. I'd been strangely looking forward to putting my new socks on. When I did, they felt amazing. That probably sounds a strange thing to say, but when you've run pretty much 4 marathons through a desert, in the same pair of socks, your feet are easily impressed. When I put my shoes on though, I couldn't work out what was going on. My shoes were far too tight. I pulled my shoes off and looked at my socks again. They were the wrong ones! How had this happened? It suddenly dawned on me. I'd trained in the socks that I'd been wearing thus far out in the desert and just before leaving the country, I'd asked Lucy to buy me a spare pair. I'd asked her to go into our local sports shop and ask them for another pair of what I'd recently bought. They know their customers inside out so I was confident they would get it right. And they had; very nearly. The socks they'd given Lucy were the updated ones of the socks I'd been running in, and had increased cushioning. Stupidly, I'd not checked them before leaving, because they looked identical. I was doubly annoyed, because not only were they useless, but also I'd carried them all around the Sahara for no reason! My shoulders were still in a lot of pain from my pack though, so I took some scissors to them, and used them as makeshift padding that I strapped direct to my shoulders. This was more to make myself feel better for having carried them to be honest, although I do think they provided some additional comfort. I then pulled on my crusty, well-worn original pair of socks with a slight sense of disappointment!

We packed up our belongings and made our way to the start. Patrick gave his customary address before setting us on our way. Patrick warned us that it was going to be windy today; thank goodness I had managed to source myself some sunglasses! As always, Duncan and I set off towards the back of the pack. I took a few gulps of my Tailwind as we started to run. The course went straight into relatively low level, undulating sand dunes. We ran into them, enjoying the terrain, the sand, the whole MDS shebang. Life was good. In my head, I was thinking there was a chance we could get this marathon done in around five hours. My marathon best was 2h58m, and Duncan's was only a little slower, and I was convinced he had a far quicker marathon than me in his legs. We both seemed to feel ok, our packs were light, so the only unknown was going to be the terrain and the weather.

As soon as we got through the sand dunes, we were met by a fierce headwind that was blowing sand straight into our faces. I pulled my buff up over my mouth and nose to stop me breathing in too much sand, and put my head down. Fairly quickly however, I began to feel both nauseous and weak. This sensation came out of nowhere and came on strong. I didn't worry; these things happen on long runs. They're typically just 'patches' and you come out of them. I carried on and didn't say anything to Duncan. 20 minutes later however, things had become worse. I reluctantly tapped Duncan on his arm, 'I'm struggling mate.' 'That's fine mate, we'll walk for a bit,' came his typically calm response. As we walked, I tried to weigh up what was causing my problems. I thought it must be a lack of fuel, so drank down a good chug of my Tailwind.

With every second that went on, however, the worse I felt. Another 20 minutes down the line and I felt I was struggling to walk. The only way I can describe it is as if I was ill. By this point, Duncan was about 50 metres ahead of me. I wanted to run to catch him up to tell him what I needed to say, but I didn't have the energy. 5 or so minutes after this, Duncan looked back and could see I was struggling. He dropped back and asked me how things were. We were 5 miles in by this point. 'I'm in the shit mate. I think I'm going to have to walk this one in. You go ahead.' Duncan wouldn't hear of it, so we continued walking for 15 to 20 minutes. The harsh wind was a constant; the sand biting into any uncovered flesh. Even after walking for 20 minutes, I didn't feel any better. I drank some more Tailwind. 'Fucking hell,' I thought to myself, 'I thought today was going to be pretty straightforward. I'm clinging on by my fingernails here.' I started trying to work out what the cut offs were, and how slow I could plod it in without being retired from the race. As I did, I took another swig of Tailwind. As the liquid entered my mouth, I noticed the briefest moment of heightened nausea. It was so fleeting I nearly missed it. As it was though, I thought I had my answer – or at least I *hoped* I had my answer. It was the Tailwind. I'm not saying there was a problem with the Tailwind (and in case any lawyers are reading this, I'm *really* not saying there was a problem with the Tailwind!) but my suspicion was that my body wasn't reacting well to it.

I pulled the bottle out from my pack strap and emptied it on the ground. I then set about drinking as much water as I could as we approached the first checkpoint. I was trying to flush my system out, and figured given how much I was sweating, it would be pretty much impossible to overhydrate. I turned to Duncan and said 'I think it's this bloody Tailwind!' At the first checkpoint, we were getting 1.5L of water, and I knew that at the second we'd be given 3L. I decided to try to get as much fluid through me as possible. We negotiated the checkpoint pretty quickly (to be honest, I don't remember a great deal about it) and got on our way.

I still felt terrible. Again I told Duncan to leave me and go on his way, but again he stuck by my side. The wind remained savage, however the terrain was by this point relatively flat. A further 20 minutes down the line, and goodness only knows how much water, I started to feel a bit better. Duncan suggested we start running, and I took him up on his suggestion. We lasted about a mile before settling back to a march. By this point, I was definitely feeling better. A further 10 minutes down the line and I was back to normal. I turned to Duncan and told him I was feeling better and he gave me a thumbs up. We put in a decent effort until we reached the 2nd checkpoint in 2hr46min. We took our 3L of water and exited in high spirits. We were just over half way, with 12 miles left.

Pretty much as soon as we exited the checkpoint though, Duncan told me he was going downhill. There was no overt cause of the problem; he was simply struggling. Just as I had been up until now, he was going through a bad patch. I felt sure he'd come through it very quickly. Except he didn't.

We alternated between running and walking for half an hour and Duncan told me he was feeling worse still. 'Go on without me, mate,' he said. 'Are you fucking kidding me?!' came my reply. It was a remarkable switch in fortunes. For the previous couple of hours, Duncan had nursed me along, but now he was in need some support. From what I could see, he actually deteriorated fairly quickly. Just as on the early part of the long day, I asked him to go in front of me so that I knew where he was. The irony was that by this point, after all my woes, I was feeling fantastic! At no point was I seriously worried about Duncan. My assessment of him was exactly the same as my assessment of me a few hours before. In the shit, but guaranteed to finish. And that was all that really mattered. We plodded on together. Every now and then Duncan would ask if I wanted to run for a bit, and I'd gladly accept. We went on like this for an hour or so. As we went, an English guy ran past and shouted 'Hey, the two Duncans!!' *Conversations back at the hotel after the completion of the event showed that Duncan and I had become quite well known on the course. For no other reason than our names on the back of our rucksacks, running side by side for the majority of the course!*

We hit checkpoint 3 which signified approximately 10km left. Duncan was still struggling although he did appear to be improving. It was a surreal period of time. We knew that we were going to finish, but we still had to get the job done; and we were both in pain. Duncan was suffering more than me, but we were both struggling. Unless you're super-elite, a marathon hurts. We ran past what looked to be an ancient monument. It was impressive, but I gave it scant attention. I had a finish line occupying my thoughts.

The run / walk itself was fairly uneventful. We were travelling through a flat but rocky area which meant that there was a thin path, approximately one foot wide, to travel along. This made over-taking difficult. Over-taking for the sake of placings wasn't on my radar at all, however over-taking in order to get the job done as soon as possible was most definitely on my wish list. I turned to my partner in crime, 'Dunc; there's about 8km to go. We can do this. We can push it in.' It was still a case of run-a-bit walk-a-bit though. I became a bit frustrated. For no reason other than the finish line felt so close.

We 'cat-and-moused' some of the London Air Ambulance team on the run in to the finish. They would overtake us, then 300 or 400m later we'd overtake them, and vice-versa. Eventually, with 2 miles to go, I consulted with Duncan and we agreed run to the finish. We overtook the London Air Ambulance guys. I gave one of the chaps a bum slap on my way past and shouted 'we're nearly there buddy!'

We ran on in a strange silence for 5-10 minutes until we saw the finish line in the distance. It was probably one mile away. There was a chap running, about 300m ahead of us, and looking round us, I saw no-one particularly close behind us. As we travelled, I realised we were gaining on the man ahead. 'We're going to do this big man,' I called out to Duncan. The inflatable gantry approached, and still we were gaining on the chap in front of us. He was close enough now that I could read his name on his number on his back. I turned to Duncan; 'mate, we don't want to be catching this guy on the line. Let's give him some space.' I can't really explain my thinking and it maybe sounds a bit patronising. I just felt that after this week-long struggle, he deserved more than being over-taken right on the line. It wasn't that sort of event. If you were mid-packing as we were, it wasn't a race, but a personal challenge. Duncan gave me a thumbs up. The finish line was less than 200m away now, and the guy in front started looking round to see who he could hear coming up behind. Reading his name bib, I shouted, 'James, we're not going to overtake you buddy. Run it in.' He raised his right fist.

40 seconds later, Duncan and I ran across the line together. We had done it. *I had done it.* I walked up to Patrick Bauer who put a medal

around my neck. I walked over to Duncan, and threw my arms around him. After all the trials and tribulations of the week, it was the most serene moment. No words were exchanged that I remember, . but time stood still for a second. We then walked out of the finishing funnel, via the webcam, where I gave a quick fist pump / cheering motion, that I instantly regretted.

We had crossed the line in 5hr47min. We exited the funnel and stood around for a minute or two, unsure what to do. The atmosphere was actually quite strange. Spirits were understandably very high, and there was lots of high-fiving, back slapping and cheering. Overall however, it was more emotional relief than overt euphoria. People were on their knees crying, sat quietly talking to themselves, and hugging. There was lots of hugging. This was the purest of moments. We would all go home to receive sincere and heartfelt congratulations and adulation from our loved ones. But right here, at the finish line, we were surrounded by people who had been in the exact same boat as us; had struggled with the same worries, fears and pain and had ultimately achieved their goal. I loved looking at the faces around me. I saw an interview with Jonny Wilkinson once where he said that if he could freeze time, he'd freeze it at the moment his drop goal was sailing through the posts in the World Cup Final. For my part, if I could freeze time, this is a moment I would love to be able to enjoy time and time again. Whilst running is technically an individual sport, this was a moment of collective team achievement. Team MDS 2018 was collectively achieving its goal. It is difficult to explain how emotion, and other peoples emotions, can take on close to a physical palpability. I've always been a big softie at heart, and being in the epicenter of people achieving their dreams, and of course, me achieving mine, was a truly wonderful feeling that I will remember for the rest of my days.

After a few minutes simply stood watching, Duncan and I thought it would be a good idea to nip back in and get some photos at the finish line. This didn't take us long so we were soon strolling back to our tent, water bottles in our arms. When we got there, we were greeted by Paul, who had enjoyed a good day out on the course. After exchanging congratulations, Paul explained that our tent wasn't actually ready and that we were all sat 'next door.' We lay in the tent with our feet up, reflecting on our achievement.

The berbers told us our tent was now ready so we decamped next door, and 20 or so minutes later we were joined by Dee. It was fantastic to see her and we enjoyed hugs all round, and listened to her tales of her day. That Dee completed the event was remarkable given she had broken her fingers on the second day; another warrior in our midst. Tent 143 was 50% complete. We all lay there enjoying the moment. Getting your just deserts doesn't happen that often in life, so this was a time to savour what we'd each done.

About half an hour later, I headed out of the tent to look for firewood. When I looked out, I saw Mark walking towards the tent. Even from the distance I was from him, I could see that he was quite emotional. I walked out to meet him with a view to carrying his water. I got to him, gave him a hug and took his water off him. We walked back to the tent and everyone congratulated our latest hero. I stayed to listen to Mark's tales before going off to get that firewood. When I returned, it wasn't long before we were joined by Jorge. More cheering all round, and hearing his tales. This left Jules and Charlotte, who completed Tent 143 around an hour later. Again, we all cheered, although louder this time because it meant we had a full-house; or tent, in this case. This was fantastic. We listened to Jules and Charlotte, who were typically understated. We all moaned to each other about how we had struggled with the wind. As we all lay there with our medals on though, I doubt any of us would have changed a single thing about the week. The hardest, most challenging, energy sapping parts were precisely the bits that made this moment so sweet.

That night, we seemed to laugh and joke all night. There was a large camp fire in the middle of the bivouac and people were sitting and standing round singing and laughing. The next day, all we had to do was a 7.7km charity stage that was compulsory, but did not count towards our final placings. They published the final results from the Marathon Des Sables 2018.

My total time of 41h00m14s put me in 424th place overall, out of 977 runners who started the race.

In reality, this mattered, and matters, very little. As Jules said, *'if someone hears you've done the MDS, they don't ask what place you came... they just shake your hand and say "fair play."'*

CHAPTER 17

Day 7 – 7.7km

I 'd been very cynical about the final day of the MDS. It seemed to me to be a publicity stunt. Which, to be fair, I guess it is. The premise is that you all wear blue t-shirts that are emblazoned with the word 'solidarité' and basically walk, in your tent groups, 7.7km to the ultimate finish. Except it's not the finish, because you already crossed the real finish the day before. It's all a bit weird.

That morning, we put on our blue t-shirts, packed up our bags, and walked to the start line. Patrick did his thing, and we all set off. Only this time, pretty much the entire field walked. The terrain was undulating with dunes. It was nice to all walk together, and have the opportunity to chat about the week. I felt a huge sense of pride in walking with my tentmates. This was Team Tent 143 all together on the course for the first time during the week. There was a party atmosphere as people took photos without the pressure of a clock timing us.

We walked along as a Tent and laughed and joked together. We told stories about our home lives and got to know each other better. Remembering it now, it was like a scene in a movie when a team of bank robbers have pulled off the perfect heist and are all enjoying the moment of their success. Out there as a group, my cynicism disappeared, and I look back glad that we did that final day. The terrain was actually pretty tough at times, with a lot of very soft, very high dunes.

Eventually, we walked straight from the edge of the desert, onto a parking lot, where a long line of buses were parked. We were directed to the appropriate bus, and hopped on board.

If I have made this final day seem like an anti-climax, it's because it was. In many ways, the MDS is one long anti-climax. Most people have earmarked the long day as their tipping point. If they can complete that, they're confident they will finish the entire race (although I nearly proved that theory wrong!). What this means is that, on completing the long day, you are euphoric, but then have the final marathon to complete, which is a bit of an anti-climax. And when that's done, and you have your medal, you then have the final 7.7km to do. Another anti-climax. Don't get me wrong though, it was all fantastic, and in many ways, helped bring you back down to earth gently.

The first thing I noticed as I got on the coach was the smell. I've been going on rugby tours for 25 years. Very grotty rugby tours, as it goes. I'd never smelt a coach like that though. Being fair, what did I expect? Put 50 people who have run over 150 miles each, and not changed clothes nor had a shower for a week, in a confined space, and it's never going to be good. The coach drove us back to civilisation.

There wasn't a huge amount of conversation on board. Just tired, weary chuckling, and a lot of smiling faces. I tried to get some sleep, but struggled. The one thing that wasn't a struggle, however, was enjoying sitting in a comfortable seat. For the previous week, the only time I had sat on a chair had been whilst waiting to see the Doc Trotters, or whilst sending emails home.

We enjoyed a few days in a hotel with the other British competitors. I phoned Lucy and enjoyed letting her know that I was in good shape, whilst relaying key details to her. It was a strange call in many ways. Lucy had been able to keep so up to date with my progress via the tracking function on the website, and also via my nightly emails that in many ways, she seemed to know more about what I had done than I did! It was fantastic to talk to her. In many ways, Lucy had been through the mill more than me during my preparations. I had willingly disappeared every weekend for hours and hours on end, leaving her with the kids. At least I had the personal goal of what I was trying to achieve. Lucy meanwhile had just been left minding the kids and keeping on top of our family lives. She was evidently incredibly proud, but also, I sensed, a touch relieved. Relieved that it was over, and that it had all been worth it.

Rooming with Duncan and Jorge, the first thing that I did when I got into the hotel was have a shower. I was in there for ages, and it was wonderful! The fine dust from the desert seemed to have completely covered me. I got out of the shower and started drying myself on a towel, only to realise I was turning the towel orange. Clearly I'd not done a good enough job, so back into the shower I went! It took a further 2 attempts, and an awful lot of scrubbing inside my ears to get myself clean.

My next task was to try to get rid of the beard I'd grown. Fortunately Paul had a beard trimmer with him so I borrowed that and before too long I was feeling fairly clean. The only issue I'd not been able to deal with was the remnants of the adhesive from the strapping that had been on my shoulders. It would take a bottle of nail-varnish remover and an awful lot of scrubbing back home to get rid of this!

During my time in the hotel, I was reminded of my fortune in not suffering any serious injury. There were a couple of people having to make their way around on crutches and others who could barely put any weight on their feet, such was the severity of their blisters. The days in the hotel were both enjoyable and useful. Enjoyable to share memories and laughs, and useful to reacclimatise to normal life. Predictably, the most enjoyable element was having a proper bed. It felt so incredibly luxurious to be lying on a pristine white sheet and soft mattress.

On the first night, there was a bit of chat suggesting we should all go out and have a few drinks to celebrate. I'm normally leading the charge for such things, but the truth was, I was shattered. I'd had a few beers throughout the day by the side of the pool, and a few more over dinner in the hotel, and was ready for bed. I was a bit disappointed in myself for not being more keen to party, but I reluctantly strolled back to my room and enjoyed a good night's sleep.

Whilst in the hotel, I had a key piece of admin from everyday life to take care of. Our son, Ted, was due to start school in the coming academic year and places were being announced on one of the days that I was in the hotel. I had registered his place with my email address so the notification would come to me. Places in our preferred school for him were tight, so we were very nervous. We had both realised that the email would come to me whilst I was away, but I'd assured Lucy that I would stay on top of things when back in the hotel. Sure enough, sat on the sofa in our suite, my phone pinged and the email came in. I told Duncan and Jorge that I needed to excuse myself to carefully read the email. I went into our room and scanned the mail. He had been granted a place at our first-choice school. This was great news. I phoned Lucy straight up to give her the news. There was a strange juxtaposition between sitting in a hotel in Morocco, nursing my feet after a life affirming adventure, and accomplishing a life-long goal, whilst also dealing with extremely important admin from back home. If anything, it showed how precious the time we had enjoyed in the desert was, when we had been able to focus on nothing other than getting from A to B.

It was a strange feeling completing the MDS. The saying goes 'never meet your heroes, you'll only be disappointed.' In many ways, completing the MDS was like meeting a hero for me. The question is, was I disappointed? The answer is; not in the slightest. The sense of quiet elation that I felt was all-consuming. I could feel it from my fingertips to my toes. I struggled for the first couple of days to understand the precise emotion I was feeling, before realising that I felt that completing the MDS granted me some kind of approval. I remember sitting on the sofa in my room in the hotel and thinking to myself 'but approval from who?!' As I strolled downstairs, it slowly dawned on me; approval from myself. I'd wanted to prove this to myself for over half my life, and now I had, I didn't give a shit what anyone else said or thought about what I'd done. What I mean by that is their praise, or condemnation even, didn't matter a jot to me. The praise that came was nice, obviously, but this was an intensely personal achievement and one only I could properly judge. Walking to the restaurant in the hotel, I remembered a poem that my cousin read out at my uncle's funeral:

> When you get what you want in your struggle for self
> and the world makes you king for a day
> Just go to the mirror and look at yourself
> and see what that man has to say
>
> For it isn't your father or mother or wife
> who judgment upon you must pass
> The fellow whose verdict counts the most in your life
> is the one staring back from the glass

Some people may think you a straight-shooting chum
and call you a wonderful guy
But the guy in the glass says you're only a bum
if you can't look him straight in the eye

He's the fellow to please never mind all the rest
for he's with you clear up to the end
And you've passed your most dangerous difficult test
if the man in the glass is your friend

You may fool the whole world down the pathway
of life and get pats on the back as you pass
But your final reward will be heartaches and
tears if you've cheated the man in the glass.

Dale Wimbrow

This poem resonated with me particularly strongly. I remember listening to my cousin, Barry, reading it out, and with the delivery of each verse, thinking 'this is it! This is the answer.' It has to be about your own view of yourself, because ultimately, you're the only person who can truly gauge the merits of your trials and tribulations. I've enjoyed successes that I haven't deserved, and similarly not enjoyed successes that I maybe did deserve.

The fantastic and awe-inspiring thing about the MDS is that it pushes people to their absolute limit and strips them back to their core. The task of getting from A to B under your own steam, but in the harshest of conditions is a challenge that takes people to a place in their mind that they've possibly never visited before. How many times in your everyday life are you pushed that hard? I think I work hard at work and in my home life, and have pushed myself hard on various physical activities over the years, but I'd never pushed myself anywhere near as hard as the MDS did. It is both humbling and exhilarating to observe and be involved in something that produces such highs and lows.

Anyone who has done any form of endurance activity that has pushed them far beyond their comfort zone knows of the patches of despondency and despair you go through during your dark times. With low blood sugar levels and exhaustion setting in, the feeling that all is lost is hard to quell. Yet it is precisely these lows that make the sense of accomplishment so unbelievably high. Without the dark, there would be no light.

During the week I saw many people in total despair and agony, and the same people also exultant when at the finish lines each day. Tears, more tears and then happy tears. The MDS is a shop window of the best in human spirit, and I am proud to say that I too was that person in absolute agony, and despair, and then ultimately in total ecstasy. Going into the desert I was genuinely unsure whether I had 'the minerals' to get the job done. The question I was asking of myself was very real, and for me personally, very scary. Proving to the man in the glass that I was equal to the challenge was an incredible moment and a feeling that will live with me forever.

I had done it. 20 years after first dreaming of it in a dingey student house in Sheffield, I had done it. And in doing so, I really had proved to my kids that you can do things you never dreamed you were capable of. *Dream until your dreams come true.*

CHAPTER 18

The Return

As I stood in baggage reclaim, I spotted the chap I had sat next to on the flight out. This was the guy who'd taken a loan out and been very definite that it was a one-time only attempt. I looked over and we caught each other's eye. We didn't say or even mouth anything at each other. Instead there was a barely perceptible nod of the head and a knowing smile. It was a strangely powerful moment. A few days before, we'd discussed our hopes with no idea how things would pan out, and then wished each other luck before not seeing each other for the remainder of the trip. Here we were, back on home soil, and both with finisher's medals. Seeing this fellow dream-chaser again neatly bookended the trip.

I claimed my bag, and bade farewell to my tent mates at the carousel. This was another slightly strange interaction. In all of the hustle and bustle of the baggage reclaim hall, it was difficult to have a conversation. I wanted to thank them all for their part in my experience, but it just wasn't possible. Instead I gave them a tight hug, told them I'd be in touch and walked through to Arrivals. I scanned the people waiting before being bowled over by Lucy as she ran over. We hugged each other hard. As she greeted me, the first thing Lucy said was she was surprised how well I looked. I explained that I'd been stuffing myself with food for the previous couple of days, whilst showering and shaving non-stop! We walked to the car; again Lucy said she was surprised how well I was walking.

In actual fact, I suffered precious few physical after-effects from my time in the desert. The blisters on my feet weren't too debilitating, and even the toes that had suffered blisters under the nails weren't offensively painful. (I ultimately lost 4 toenails when I returned, but that's not too bad). I'd been worried about chafing in advance of the trip, but this hadn't been too much of a problem either. My shoulders were bruised from the pressure points on my pack, but again, this wasn't anything to write home about. Something was different inside though. I don't really know how to describe it, other than to say it felt like I'd used up something out in the desert that was quite probably a one-time-only expenditure. I felt different. For some reason, I felt purer; like I had banished some demons.

The time in the car driving back home was useful as it enabled me to give Lucy a day by day account of how things had gone. She said that I'd be amazed by how much interest there had been back home, and that everyone was over the moon that I'd done it. Being super organised, Lucy had brought me a feast for the journey home, but I didn't really feel like it. I think I'd either over-eaten in the hotel, or shrunk my stomach whilst in the desert; either way, I didn't feel like eating too much. *(When I got home, I weighed myself and found that I was 16lbs lighter than when I left. Allowing for the 2 days in an all-inclusive hotel following the race, I suspect I'd lost around one and a half stone in a little over a week. Not bad going, as my own version of the slim-fast-plan!)*

We arrived home and I saw my mum. I gave her a brief version of the story I had just given Lucy in the car but by this point I was pretty tired and in need of my bed. Before turning in though, there was one very important last job. It was Millie's birthday the next day, and I'd promised her a medal as a present. My mum said that she was still awake. I excitedly went into her room and she jumped out of bed and flung her arms around me.

"Daaddddyyyy!"
"Hello sweetheart; how are you?"
"I'm good thank you daddy. You beat the camel!!"
"I know! And look what I got for you."
"My medal!!! Thank you daddy!! I just knew you would win."
"I didn't win Millie!"
"Yes you did daddy."

It comes to something when you need a 6-year-old to tell you the way of the world. She was right; I had won. I'd won in my search of self. I hugged her close and hard and told her how much the messages she had sent had meant to me. She smiled, gave me kiss good night and I put my medal on her bedside table with my mission firmly accomplished. *Dream until your dreams come true.*

EPILOGUE

I am finishing writing this book around 6 months after returning from the desert. Since returning, I've barely run. I have bought a road bike and am trying to 'get into' cycling, but it's not pushing my buttons the way running does. The truth is, I've really struggled for motivation since I have returned. I cannot motivate myself to go out and run a 'regular' 10km, or even a marathon to be honest. In my mind, what's the point? I may have set the bar too high in terms of what gets my juices flowing, but I'm hoping this will recalibrate over time. In many ways, the MDS was my Everest.

When I returned, the one question I was asked the most was 'what are you going to do next?' The truth is, I don't really know, and it's got me down a bit. I have loved having more time with my family, and not cramming so much into the weekends with Saturday and Sunday both being punctuated by long runs. The reality is though, for quite a few years the MDS was defining both my behaviours and my identity, and now I don't have that, I feel a bit lost. I can see how people can struggle when they retire from work, and am finding myself looking around trying to replace the anchor point that the goal provided. I've felt like I'm drifting, and I have realised that I put all of my efforts into preparing for what would happen when I was out in the desert, and no thought into preparing for what would happen when I returned. This may sound very strange, but I think my return could have been easier had I failed. I realise now that my claims that it was a one-time-only attempt were not true. Had I not succeeded, I would have been straight on the phone trying to secure a place for the following year. Now that I have succeeded, what am I to do now?

Writing this now, I don't want to stop typing. I don't want to close my laptop because I don't want the story to end. I have absolutely no desire to take on the desert again, but I also don't feel totally ready to say goodbye. In many ways it feels like the end of a romance between me and the Sahara. It's not like she dumped me, or I dumped her, and there's no-one else involved, but our relationship has run its course. I don't know what I will do, but I'll move on. I'll find something else. As a well-known song goes, 'Never mind, I'll find someone like you.' In the meantime, I offer a sincere and heartfelt thank you to the Marathon Des Sables; you were everything I hoped and dreamed you would be.

TECHNICAL DETAIL

I thought it may be useful for me to set out what my full kit list with comments, along with what I felt I did right, and what I felt I did wrong both in preparation and out in the desert.

Full Kit List

Item	Comments	Recommend
Shoes – Brooks Pure Cadence	These were perfect. I didn't go the size up and they were absolutely fantastic. These are traditional road shoes and they were great. They were trashed, by the end, mind	Yes

	and went straight in the bin when I returned!	
Socks – Hilly Energise Compression long socks	These long socks provided just the right amount of cushioning whilst also giving protection against the sun. Perfect.	Yes
Gaters – Myracekit	These were spot on. No issues at all.	Yes
Shorts – Asics 5 inch lined	Absolutely fantastic. These are my favourite shorts and caused me no issues whatsoever. Perfect.	Yes
Top – Raidlight Desert Running Top	This did the job perfectly. I went for the white which I hoped would reflect the heat a touch. Whether it did or not, I don't know – but it certainly showed the dirt!	Yes
Cap – OR Sun Runner Cap	Nothing majorly exciting nor sexy, but it did all I asked of it.	Yes
Compression leggings – Skins	I wore these at night time and was very glad I took them given the temperature.	Yes
Compression vest – Nike	Just like the leggings, I wore these at night time to combat the cold. I'd definitely recommend some 'night wear.'	Yes
Down jacket – Haglofs Essens	This was essential at night time in the camp	Yes

	and also on the long stage. It shrinks down really small but is very warm.	
Buff	This is a must. It serves as a hat when it's cold, a mask when there's a sand storm, and sunblock around your neck.	Yes
Watch – Garmin Forerunner 235	This was great accept the battery wasn't up to tracking the long day. If I had my time again I'd get a watch with a better battery	No
Sunglasses – Foam Padded Xtreme Goggle/Glasses	I bought these glasses of Amazon and they were fantastic. They had a foam padding around the edge that effectively sealed them to your face meaning no sand could get in. It's just a shame that I lost them!	Yes
Sleeping bag – Yeti Zero	This was expensive, but worth it, It shrinks down very small yet still provides decent warmth	Yes
Sleeping bag liner – RAB Silk	I was grateful for this as it gets very cold at night time!	Yes
Sleeping mat – Thermarest Neoair	This wouldn't stay inflated so was virtually useless. I should have taken a solid mat	No

Pillow – Klymit Pillow X55G	This kept me comfortable whilst shrinking down small when deflated. Perfect.	Yes
Backpack – Salomon Slab20	Despite being great whilst training, this gave me untold problems in the desert due to the pressure spots. Everyone I saw with the same pack had the same problems. If there was only one thing I could change about my kit it would be this.	No
Water bottles	I went with solid rather than soft bottles as I was concerned about them puncturing. The ones I took were dictated by size; these were the only solid bottles that fit	Yes
Cooking pot	Did the job. Perfect.	Yes
Stove	Just like the pot. It did the job	Yes
Fuel tablets	These did the job but with hindsight I wouldn't have bothered, would have saved the weight and just used kindling that's readily available around the camp	No
MDS Mandatory Items	I bought the pack from Myracekit which did the job perfectly. You hope you don't need most of it!	Yes

Spare laces and cable ties	I put these in 'just in case' and used all of them at various points. I'd definitely recommend taking some.	Yes
Hairbands	I took some hairbands and used these as a means of attaching my number to my front and pack, but with flexibility. I looped them through the holes in my number and safety pinned them to my front and pack. It worked really well	Yes
Phone – iPhone 6s	I took this predominantly as a camera but also as a music player. The only issue was the notoriously poor iPhone battery.	Yes
Powerblock	This was essential to charge both my watch and phone.	Yes
Spare strapping	I took this 'just in case' but needn't have bothered. The Doc Trotters will give you strapping when you're out there so there was no need.	Yes
Two thin sponges	I took these to serve as padding if required. They were really useful, and barely weigh anything	Yes
Casio watch	I took this so that I	No

	could use it as a timer to remind me to drink but needn't have bothered. Out in the heat I didn't need reminding!	
MP3 player x2	I took two very light MP3 players as I was paranoid about having no music to run to given I always run to music at home. These were as back up to my phone and were very light, but I didn't use them in the end so shouldn't have bothered taking and carrying them.	No
Headphones x2	I took 2 pairs of wired headphones in case one failed, which they did. It was definitely better to take wired rather than wireless which would have needed charging. In reality though I could have done without them, as I barely listened to music whilst out in the desert.	No
Suncream – 2x Tingerlaat SPF50 20ml	This is incredible stuff. You barely need any of it on your skin and it is total sunblock.	Yes
Gurny Goo	Gurny Goo is anti-chafing lubricant that is absolutely essential out in the desert. I didn't get any	Yes

	chafing at all which is testament to how good this stuff is.	

What I got right:

- My kit was on the money. Despite my panic over my shoes on day one, these stood up to it well. I would recommend each bit of running kit I wore

- My food whilst out there. I panicked a lot about my nutrition whilst out in the desert. Did I have enough? Would I be hungry? As it was, I had the perfect amount of food and never felt overtly hungry, whilst also not carrying too much weight that I didn't eat.

- My trainers. My shoes were such a major source of concern. I fretted about these more than anything, but ultimately I got it right. Other than the freak occurrence of the thorn within the first km, that never repeated itself, my shoes were absolutely perfect. I didn't go a size up as a lot of people recommend, and went with regular road shoes that I wear all the time at home. The lack of blisters at the end were testament to me getting it right.

- I took the salt tablets religiously and as a result barely suffered with cramp. As someone who has always suffered badly with cramp whilst running, this was a revelation. I've now upped my salt content in my regular diet as a result.

- My training was broadly right. (see caveat on 'what I got wrong!'). Running close to 100 miles in a week was key to both toughen up my body and also give me the mental confidence to take the challenge on. Crucially though, I built my mileage up steadily; typically not increasing my mileage by more than 10% each week.

- My tent mates. They were top class and made the week so much more enjoyable. Granted this wasn't actually something 'I got right,' but they deserve a special mention. Thank you to Paul, Mark, Jorge, Dee, Duncan, Jules & Charlotte. You are incredible people, and were the best companions I could have asked for.

What I got wrong:

- My backpack. The biggest thing I got wrong was my pack. It was so incredibly uncomfortable, and a different pack would have made my week so much more enjoyable. I'll never understand how the pressure points didn't present themselves before the desert itself, despite the hundreds of miles I put in wearing the pack, but everyone else with the Salomon Peak 20 back pack suffered the same fate. I would strongly advise against taking it.
- My sleeping mat was rubbish. I had a Thermarest inflatable mat, and it just didn't perform. I wish I had taken a solid mat that didn't rely on air.
- Insufficient walking in my training. Walking is a different gait to running and uses different muscles, and you do **a lot** of walking in the MDS. I hadn't prepared for this at all. I should have spent 7 – 10 days spread throughout my training, walking all day, to toughen my body up.
- I worried too much beforehand and during the first day. It's easy with hindsight to say 'I shouldn't have worried so much,' but I really shouldn't.

I have a theory that if you can run a 5km, you can run a 10km. And if you can run a 10km, you can run a half marathon. If you can run a half marathon, you can definitely run a full marathon. And if you can run a marathon, you can definitely run and complete the MDS. Granted, it's all stepping stones, but I passionately believe this is possible.

If you've read this, it's probably because the MDS has captured your imagination and you may be either seriously or loosely considering taking on the challenge. What I would say is don't delay; chase your dream. Do it. Do it. Because, you CAN do it. You can definitely do it. And the reason I can say this with such confidence is because the MDS isn't about your legs; it's about your head. If you think you can do it, you almost certainly can.

PHOTOS

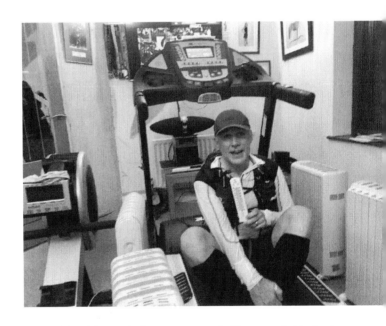

Acclimatising to the heat on my treadmill surrounded by heaters

All my kit set out before departure

Walking to the start line

Tent 143 with most of us still in our sleeping bags

Foot preparation!

Sunrise over the bivouac

An MDS toilet. You stretch a bag over the frame. It's not the most enjoyable experience.

Cooking dinner

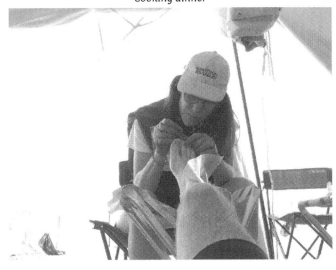

One of the Doc Trotter team lancing the blisters under my toenails after Day 2

The boulder field that caused me such grief towards the end of Day 3

The fabled can of Coca-Cola on the rest day after the long stage

The two Duncans...

Preparing to run through a sand storm

Me & Duncan just after we crossed the final finish line

At the finish line with Duncan

Tent 143 on the final day.

In the tent with the medal I'd been dreaming of for 20 years

The medal on Millie's bedside table ready for her birthday (along with a pink camel I bought her at the airport!). Mission accomplished.

Printed in Great Britain
by Amazon